Library Association of
Warehouse Point
Connecticut

WITHDRAWN

SOME THINGS STRANGE AND SINISTER

OTHER BOOKS EDITED BY
JOAN KAHN

The Edge of the Chair
Some Things Dark and Dangerous
Some Things Fierce and Fatal

SOME THINGS STRANGE AND SINISTER

Edited by
Joan Kahn

Harper & Row, Publishers
New York   Evanston   San Francisco   London

SOME THINGS STRANGE AND SINISTER
Copyright © 1973 by Joan Kahn
All rights reserved. No part of this book may be used or reproduced in any manner whatsoever without written permission except in the case of brief quotations embodied in critical articles and reviews. Printed in the United States of America. For information address Harper & Row, Publishers, Inc., 10 East 53rd Street, New York, N.Y. 10022. Published simultaneously in Canada by Fitzhenry & Whiteside Limited, Toronto.
Library of Congress Catalog Card Number: 72-9871
Trade Standard Book Number: 06-023086-X
Harpercrest Standard Book Number: 06-023087-8
FIRST EDITION

Grateful acknowledgment is made as follows for the copyrighted material reprinted in this collection.

"The Lamp," by Agatha Christie. Reprinted from *The Hound of Death and Other Stories* by Agatha Christie, by permission of The Hamlyn Publishing Group.

"Nerves," by Guy de Maupassant. Copyright 1924 and renewed 1952 by Alfred A. Knopf, Inc. Reprinted from *Complete Novels and Stories of Guy de Maupassant,* translated by Ernest Boyd, by permission of Random House, Inc., and Cassell & Co., Ltd.

"Thus I Refute Beelzy," by John Collier. Copyright 1940, 1967 by John Collier. Reprinted by permission of The Harold Matson Company, Inc.

"Keeping His Promise," by Algernon Blackwood. Reprinted from *The Empty House* by Algernon Blackwood, by permission of The Public Trustees and the Garnstone Press.

"The House," by André Maurois. Copyright © 1967 by Washington Square Press, Inc. Reprinted from *The Collected Stories of André Maurois,* translated by Adrienne Foulke, by permission of the author and the author's agents, Scott Meredith Literary Agency, Inc., 580 Fifth Avenue, New York, New York 10036.

"The Call of the Hand," by Louis Golding. Copyright 1935 by Louis Golding. Copyright © 1963 by Barclays Bank of England. Reprinted from *This Wanderer* by Louis Golding, by permission of Holt, Rinehart and Winston, Inc., and R. Harben Literary Agency.

"The Story of the Late Mr. Elvesham," by H. G. Wells. Reprinted from *The Short Stories of H. G. Wells* by permission of the Estate of H. G. Wells.

"The Strange Occurrences Connected With Captain John Russell," by Neil Bell. Reprinted from *Modern Reading,* edited by Reginald Moore, by permission of the Estate of the late Neil Bell.

"The Book," by Margaret Irwin. Reprinted by permission of A. D. Peters and Company.

"The Cocoon," by John B. L. Goodwin. Copyright 1946 by Story Magazine, Inc. Reprinted from *Story* Magazine, by permission of Scholastic Magazines, Inc.

"The Empty Schoolroom," by Pamela Hansford Johnson. Reprinted from *That Uncertain Feeling,* edited by Kay Dick and Jeremy Scott, by permission of David Higham Associates, Ltd.

to Ely and Elsie

Contents

INTRODUCTION ix

THE LAMP
    by *Agatha Christie* 1

NERVES
    by *Guy de Maupassant* 12

THUS I REFUTE BEELZY
    by *John Collier* 19

KEEPING HIS PROMISE
    by *Algernon Blackwood* 26

THE HOUSE
    by *André Maurois* 46

THE CALL OF THE HAND
    by *Louis Golding* 50

THE DREAM WOMAN
    by *W. Wilkie Collins* 69

THE STORY OF THE LATE MR. ELVESHAM
    by *H. G. Wells* 102

THE STRANGE OCCURRENCES CONNECTED WITH
    CAPTAIN JOHN RUSSELL
    by *Neil Bell* 125

THE BOOK
    by Margaret Irwin   146

DRACULA'S GUEST
    by Bram Stoker   168

THE COCOON
    by John B. L. Goodwin   185

THE EMPTY SCHOOLROOM
    by Pamela Hansford Johnson   208

THE GHOST OF WASHINGTON
    Anonymous   229

Introduction

I don't think I've ever actually seen a ghost, though I wouldn't mind seeing one. And of course, I can't be absolutely sure I haven't. Because I don't suppose you can always recognize a ghost. I doubt that all ghosts wear long white sheets or carry their heads around in their hands, or clank about in chains, or are clearly transparent. I mean some ghosts may have those traditional attributes, but *some* of them may not. For all I know, that rather plump, slightly sweaty woman sitting next to me on the bus, with a stuffed shopping bag at her feet, might not be a real woman at all. *I* might be the only person who could see her (and even smell her) and everyone else on the bus might think the seat next to me was empty. And unless someone came to sit on what looked like an empty seat and the woman *and* her shopping bag disappeared, poof, just as the non-ghost-viewer sat down—how could I tell?

We just can't ever be sure about ghosts. Of course we're sure *we're* solid, living human beings. We can stub our toes, or sneeze, and see ourselves in the mirror, and drink a glass of water without having it splash straight through us onto the floor. We're not *ghosts*, we're a bunch of atoms who happen to be shaped into a certain individual shape in a certain place at a certain time. *We're* as real as anything—at the moment, at least.

But occasionally, we join the company of imaginative writers who make us wonder just how real we may be. As they explore some of the meanings of reality, of substance and non-substance, of fact and fantasy, they can give us goose pimples. (And that's an odd phrase, now that I consider it, but let's not consider it *too* much.)

In this book a number of very good writers have produced some deliciously unnerving stories about people and places that may not even exist. Or did they? And do they?

If you're very timid and easily frightened, *please* don't read this book. But if you are brave and imaginative and are willing to come on some fascinating journeys in excellent company, then start reading. But perhaps not when you're alone in the house, just in case.

J.K.

The Lamp

by Agatha Christie

It was thought that a child's ghost haunted the place.

It was undoubtedly an old house. The whole square was old, with that disapproving dignified old age often met with in a cathedral town. But No. 19 gave the impression of an elder among elders; it had a veritable patriarchal solemnity; it towered grayest of the gray, haughtiest of the haughty, chillest of the chill. Austere, forbidding, and stamped with that particular desolation attaching to all houses that have been long untenanted, it reigned above the other dwellings.

In any other town it would have been freely labeled "haunted," but Weyminster was averse from ghosts and considered them hardly respectable except as the appanage of a "county family." So No. 19 was never alluded to as a haunted house; but nevertheless it remained, year after year, "To be Let or Sold."

Mrs. Lancaster looked at the house with approval as she drove up with the talkative house agent, who was in an unusually hilarious mood at the idea of getting No. 19 off his books. He inserted the key in the door without ceasing his appreciative comments.

"How long has the house been empty?" inquired Mrs. Lancaster, cutting short his flow of language rather brusquely.

Mr. Raddish (of Raddish and Foplow) became slightly confused.

"Er—er—some time," he remarked blandly.

"So I should think," said Mrs. Lancaster drily.

The dimly lighted hall was chill with a sinister chill. A more imaginative woman might have shivered, but this woman happened to be eminently practical. She was tall with much dark brown hair just tinged with gray and rather cold blue eyes.

She went over the house from attic to cellar, asking a pertinent question from time to time. The inspection over, she came back into one of the front rooms looking out on the square and faced the agent with a resolute mien.

"What is the matter with the house?"

Mr. Raddish was taken by surprise.

"Of course, an unfurnished house is always a little gloomy," he parried feebly.

"Nonsense," said Mrs. Lancaster. "The rent is ridiculously low for such a house—purely nominal. There must be some reason for it. I suppose the house is haunted?"

Mr. Raddish gave a nervous little start but said nothing.

Mrs. Lancaster eyed him keenly. After a few moments she spoke again.

"Of course that is all nonsense, I don't believe in

The Lamp

ghosts or anything of that sort, and personally it is no deterrent to my taking the house; but servants, unfortunately, are very credulous and easily frightened. It would be kind of you to tell me exactly what—what thing *is* supposed to haunt this place."

"I—er—really don't know," stammered the house agent.

"I am sure you must," said the lady quietly. "I cannot take the house without knowing. What was it? A murder?"

"Oh! no," cried Mr. Raddish, shocked by the idea of anything so alien to the respectability of the square. "It's—it's—only a child."

"A child?"

"Yes.

"I don't know the story exactly," he continued reluctantly. "Of course, there are all kinds of different versions, but I believe that about thirty years ago a man going by the name of Williams took No. 19. Nothing was known of him; he kept no servants; he had no friends; he seldom went out in the daytime. He had one child, a little boy. After he had been there about two months, he went up to London, and had barely set foot in the metropolis before he was recognized as being a man 'wanted' by the police on some charge—exactly what, I do not know. But it must have been a grave one, because, sooner than give himself up, he shot himself. Meanwhile, the child lived on here, alone in the house. He had food for a little time, and he waited day after day for his father's return. Unfortunately, it had been impressed upon him that he was never under any circumstances to go out of the house or to speak to anyone. He was a weak, ailing, little creature, and did not dream of disobeying this command. In the night, the neighbors, not knowing that his father had gone away, often heard him sobbing in the awful loneliness and desolation of the empty house."

Mr. Raddish paused.

"And—er—the child starved to death," he concluded, in the same tones as he might have announced that it had just begun to rain.

"And it is the child's ghost that is supposed to haunt the place?" asked Mrs. Lancaster.

"It is nothing of consequence really," Mr. Raddish hastened to assure her. "There's nothing *seen*, not *seen*, only people say, ridiculous, of course, but they do say they hear—the child—crying, you know."

Mrs. Lancaster moved towards the front door.

"I like the house very much," she said. "I shall get nothing as good for the price. I will think it over and let you know."

"It really looks very cheerful, doesn't it, Papa?"

Mrs. Lancaster surveyed her new domain with approval. Gay rugs, well-polished furniture, and many knickknacks, had quite transformed the gloomy aspect of No. 19.

She spoke to a thin, bent old man with stooping shoulders and a delicate mystical face. Mr. Winburn did not resemble his daughter; indeed no greater contrast could be imagined than that presented by her resolute practicalness and his dreamy abstraction.

"Yes," he answered with a smile, "no one would dream the house was haunted."

"Papa, don't talk nonsense! On our first day too."

Mr. Winburn smiled.

The Lamp

"Very well, my dear, we will agree that there are no such things as ghosts."

"And please," continued Mrs. Lancaster, "don't say a word before Geoff. He's so imaginative."

Geoff was Mrs. Lancaster's little boy. The family consisted of Mr. Winburn, his widowed daughter, and Geoffrey.

Rain had begun to beat against the window—pitter-patter, pitter-patter.

"Listen," said Mr. Winburn. "Is it not like little footsteps?"

"It's more like rain," said Mrs. Lancaster, with a smile.

"But *that, that* is a footstep," cried her father, bending forward to listen.

Mrs. Lancaster laughed outright.

"That's Geoff coming downstairs."

Mr. Winburn was obliged to laugh too. They were having tea in the hall, and he had been sitting with his back to the staircase. He now turned his chair round to face it.

Little Geoffrey was coming down, rather slowly and sedately, with a child's awe of a strange place. The stairs were of polished oak, uncarpeted. He came across and stood by his mother. Mr. Winburn gave a slight start. As the child was crossing the floor, he distinctly heard another pair of footsteps on the stairs, as of someone following Geoffrey. Dragging footsteps, curiously painful they were. Then he shrugged his shoulders incredulously. "The rain, no doubt," he thought.

"I'm looking at the spongecakes," remarked Geoff

with the admirably detached air of one who points out an interesting fact.

His mother hastened to comply with the hint.

"Well, Sonny, how do you like your new home?" she asked.

"Lots," replied Geoffrey with his mouth generously filled. "Pounds and pounds and pounds." After this last assertion, which was evidently expressive of the deepest contentment, he relapsed into silence, only anxious to remove the spongecake from the sight of man in the least time possible.

Having bolted the last mouthful, he burst forth into speech.

"Oh! Mummy, there's attics here, Jane says; and can I go at once and *eggz*plore them? And there might be a secret door. Jane says there isn't, but I think there must be, and, anyhow, I know there'll be *pipes, water pipes* (with a face full of ecstasy) and can I play with them, and, oh! can I go and see the boi-i-ler?" He spun out the last word with such evident rapture that his grandfather felt ashamed to reflect that this peerless delight of childhood only conjured up to his imagination the picture of hot water that wasn't hot, and heavy and numerous plumber's bills.

"We'll see about the attics tomorrow, darling," said Mrs. Lancaster. "Suppose you fetch your bricks and build a nice house, or an engine."

"Don't want to build an 'ouse."

"House."

"House, or h'engine h'either."

"Build a boiler," suggested his grandfather.

Geoffrey brightened.

"With pipes?"

"Yes, lots of pipes."

Geoffrey ran away happily to fetch his bricks.

The rain was still falling. Mr. Winburn listened. Yes, it must have been the rain he had heard; but it did sound like footsteps.

He had a queer dream that night.

He dreamt that he was walking through a town, a great city it seemed to him. But it was a children's city; there were no grown-up people there, nothing but children, crowds of them. In his dream they all rushed to the stranger crying: "Have you brought him?" It seemed that he understood what they meant and shook his head sadly. When they saw this, the children turned away and began to cry, sobbing bitterly.

The city and the children faded away and he awoke to find himself in bed, but the sobbing was still in his ears. Though wide awake, he heard it distinctly; and he remembered that Geoffrey slept on the floor below, while this sound of a child's sorrow descended from above. He sat up and struck a match. Instantly the sobbing ceased.

Mr. Winburn did not tell his daughter of the dream or its sequel. That it was no trick of his imagination, he was convinced; indeed soon afterwards he heard it again in the daytime. The wind was howling in the chimney, but *this* was a separate sound—distinct, unmistakable: pitiful little heartbroken sobs.

He found out too that he was not the only one to hear them. He overheard the housemaid saying to the parlormaid that she "didn't think as that there nurse was kind to Master Geoffrey. She'd 'eard 'im crying 'is little 'eart out only that very morning." Geoffrey had come down to breakfast and lunch beaming with health and happiness; and Mr. Winburn knew that it was not

Geoff who had been crying, but that other child whose dragging footsteps had startled him more than once.

Mrs. Lancaster alone never heard anything. Her ears were not perhaps attuned to catch sounds from another world.

Yet one day she also received a shock.

"Mummy," said Geoffrey plaintively. "I wish you'd let me play with that little boy."

Mrs. Lancaster looked up from her writing table with a smile.

"What little boy, dear?"

"I don't know his name. He was in a attic, sitting on the floor crying, but he ran away when he saw me. I suppose he was *shy* (with slight contempt), not like a *big* boy, and then, when I was in the nursery building, I saw him standing in the door watching me build, and he looked so awful lonely and as though he wanted to play wiv me. I said: 'Come and build a h'engine,' but he didn't say nothing, just looked as—as though he saw a lot of chocolates, and his mummy had told him not to touch them." Geoff sighed, sad personal reminiscences evidently recurring to him. "But when I asked Jane who he was and told her I wanted to play wiv him, she said there wasn't no little boy in the 'ouse and not to tell naughty stories. I don't love Jane at all."

Mrs. Lancaster got up.

"Jane was right. There was no little boy."

"But I saw him. Oh! Mummy, do let me play wiv him, he did look so awful lonely and unhappy. I *do* want to do something to 'make him better.'"

Mrs. Lancaster was about to speak again, but her father shook his head.

"Geoff," he said very gently, "that poor little boy *is*

The Lamp

lonely, and perhaps you may do something to comfort him; but you must find out how by yourself—like a puzzle—do you see?"

"Is it because I am getting *big* I must do it all my lone?"

"Yes, because you are getting big."

As the boy left the room, Mrs. Lancaster turned to her father impatiently.

"Papa, this is absurd. To encourage the boy to believe the servants' idle tales!"

"No servant has told the child anything," said the old man gently. "He's seen—what I *hear*, what I could see perhaps if I were his age."

"But it's such nonsense! Why don't I see it or hear it?"

Mr. Winburn smiled, a curiously tired smile, but did not reply.

"Why?" repeated his daughter. "And why did you tell him he could help the—the—thing? It's—it's all so impossible."

The old man looked at her with his thoughtful glance.

"Why not?" he said. "Do you remember these words:

> *What Lamp has Destiny to guide*
> *Her little Children stumbling in the Dark?*
> *'A Blind Understanding,' Heaven replied.*

"Geoffrey has that—a blind understanding. All children possess it. It is only as we grow older that we lose it, that we cast it away from us. Sometimes, when we are quite old, a faint gleam comes back to us, but the Lamp burns brightest in childhood. That is why I think Geoffrey may help."

"I don't understand," murmured Mrs. Lancaster feebly.

"No more do I. That—that child is in trouble and wants—to be set free. But how? I do not know, but—it's awful to think of it—sobbing its heart out—a *child*."

A month after this conversation Geoffrey fell very ill. The east wind had been severe, and he was not a strong child. The doctor shook his head and said that it was a grave case. To Mr. Winburn he divulged more and confessed that the case was quite hopeless. "The child would never have lived to grow up, under any circumstances," he added. "There has been serious lung trouble for a long time."

It was when nursing Geoff that Mrs. Lancaster became aware of that—other child. At first the sobs were an indistinguishable part of the wind, but gradually they became more distinct, more unmistakable. Finally she heard them in moments of dead calm: a child's sobs—dull, hopeless, heartbroken.

Geoff grew steadily worse and in his delirium he spoke of the "little boy" again and again. "I do want to help him get away, I do!" he cried.

Succeeding the delirium there came a state of lethargy. Geoffrey lay very still, hardly breathing, sunk in oblivion. There was nothing to do but wait and watch. Then there came a still night, clear and calm, without one breath of wind.

Suddenly the child stirred. His eyes opened. He looked past his mother towards the open door. He tried to speak and she bent down to catch the half-breathed words.

"All right, I'm comin'," he whispered; then he sank back.

The mother felt suddenly terrified; she crossed the

The Lamp

room to her father. Somewhere near them the other child was laughing. Joyful, contented, triumphant, the silvery laughter echoed through the room.

"I'm frightened; I'm frightened," she moaned.

He put his arm round her protectingly. A sudden gust of wind made them both start, but it passed swiftly and left the air quiet as before.

The laughter had ceased and there crept to them a faint sound, so faint as hardly to be heard, but growing louder till they could distinguish it. Footsteps—light footsteps, swiftly departing.

Pitter-patter, pitter-patter, they ran—those well-known halting little feet. Yet—surely—now *other* footsteps suddenly mingled with them, moving with a quicker and a lighter tread.

With one accord they hastened to the door.

Down, down, down, past the door, close to them, pitter-patter, pitter-patter, went the unseen feet of the little children *together*.

Mrs. Lancaster looked up wildly.

"There are *two* of them—*two*!"

Gray with sudden fear, she turned towards the cot in the corner, but her father restrained her gently, and pointed away.

"There," he said simply.

Pitter-patter, pitter-patter—fainter and fainter.

And then—silence.

Nerves

by Guy de Maupassant

TRANSLATED BY ERNEST BOYD

"I also noticed that the young girl kept a glove on her left hand, during meals."

The diners slowly entered the big hotel dining room and took their places. The waiters refrained from hurrying, so as to give the latecomers a chance, and avoid the trouble of handing the dishes round a second time. The old bathers, the habitués, whose season was almost over, looked intently at the door whenever it opened, to see what new faces might appear.

That is the chief amusement of watering places. One goes to dinner to inspect each day's new arrivals, to guess what they are, what they do and what they think. We all have a vague wish to meet pleasant people, to make agreeable acquaintances, even to meet with a love adventure. In this jostling life, neighbors, strangers, assume considerable importance. Curiosity is aroused, sympathy awaits its opportunity, and the desire to make friends is always alert.

We cherish dislikes for a week and friendship for a month; people are seen with different eyes when viewed through the medium of a meeting at a watering place. After an hour's chat in the evening after dinner, under the trees of the park where the healing spring bubbles, superior intelligence and outstanding merits are suddenly discovered in human beings, but a month later we have completely forgotten the new friends we found so charming at the first meeting.

Permanent and serious ties are also formed there sooner than elsewhere. You meet every day and soon get to know one another, and growing affection is mingled with the pleasure and unrestraint of longstanding intimacy. You never forget the sweetness and compassion of early friendship, the first conversations which end in the discovery of a soul, the first glances charged with questions and replies, and secret thoughts not yet uttered by human lips, or the first heartfelt confidence, the delightful feeling of opening our hearts to those who seem to open theirs to us in return.

And the sadness of watering places, the monotony of days all alike, make this blossoming of affection all the more complete.

Well, that evening, as on every other evening, we were waiting for the arrival of newcomers.

Only two arrived, a man and woman—father and daughter—but they looked very unusual. They immediately reminded me of some of Edgar Poe's characters; and yet they had a charm, the charm of unhappiness; and I imagined them as the victims of fate. The man was tall and thin, rather bent, with hair that was too white for his age; his bearing and his person betrayed the grave, austere manners peculiar to Protestants. The daughter, aged about twenty-four or five, was short, very thin, very pale, and seemed worn out, tired, and overwrought. Occasionally you meet people who seem too weak for the tasks and needs of daily life, too weak to move about, to walk, to do any of the daily round. The young thing was rather pretty, with a transparent, spiritual beauty. She ate extremely slowly as if she could hardly move her arms.

It was surely she who had come to take the waters.

They sat facing me, on the other side of the table, and I noticed at once that the father had a very curious nervous contraction. Every time he wanted to reach anything, his hand made a rapid hooklike movement, a kind of wild zigzag, before it could get hold of what it wanted. After a few minutes this twitching tired me to such an extent that I turned my head away so as not to see it.

I also noticed that the young girl kept a glove on her left hand, during meals.

After dinner I went for a stroll in the grounds of the bathing establishment. We were in the little Auvergne village of Châtel-Guyon, hidden in a gorge at the foot of the high range from which so many boiling springs flow, arising from the deep bed of extinct volcanoes. Over there, above our heads, the cones, extinct craters, raised their stunted heads above the rest of the long mountainous chain, for Châtel-Guyon lies at the beginning of the land of the Dôme.

Farther away lies the country of the peaks, and farther still the country of the Plombs.

The Puy-de-Dôme is the highest of the volcanic ones, the Pic of Sancy the highest of the rocky peaks, and the Plomb de Cantal is the highest point of the gigantic mass of Cantal.

It was a very warm evening. I was walking up and down the shady raised path that overlooked the grounds and listening to the music of the casino when I caught sight of the father and daughter slowly coming in my direction. I bowed as one bows to one's hotel companions at a watering place; and the man, stopping, asked me:

"Could you suggest a short walk, sir, pleasant and, if possible, not hilly? Forgive me for bothering you."

I offered to take them to the valley through which the little river flows, a deep valley forming a narrow gorge between two steep, craggy, wooded slopes. They accepted my offer.

And, of course, we talked of the virtue of the waters.

"Oh," he said, "my daughter has a curious illness whose origin is a mystery. She suffers from unaccountable nervous attacks. Sometimes she is supposed to be suffering from heart disease, sometimes from a liver attack, and sometimes from disease of the spine. Now this complicated malady with its numerous forms and numerous modes of attack, is placed in the stomach, the great center and great regulator of the body. That's why we are here. For my part, I think it is nervous trouble. In any case, it is very sad."

Immediately I remembered the violent twitching of his hand and asked him:

"But is it not due to heredity? Are you not suffering from your nerves?"

He replied quietly: "Me? . . . Certainly not . . . my nerves have always been very steady. . . ."

Then suddenly, after a pause, he continued:

"Ah! you mean the contraction of my hand every

time I want to take hold of anything? That is the result of a terrible experience I had. Just imagine, this child has been buried alive!"

I could only utter an "ah," full of surprise and emotion.

He continued:

"This is the story, a quite simple one. For some time Juliette had suffered from severe heart attacks. We believed that her heart was diseased, and were prepared for the worst.

"One day she was carried into the house cold, lifeless, dead. She had fallen unconscious in the garden. The doctor certified that life was extinct. I kept watch for two nights and a day; with my own hands I laid her in the coffin which I accompanied to the cemetery, where it was placed in the family vault, in Lorraine in the depth of the country.

"It had been my wish to have her buried with her jewelry, bracelets, necklaces, rings—all of the presents I had given her—and dressed in her first ball dress.

"You may easily imagine my state of mind when I got back home. She was the only one left, for my wife had been dead for many years. Half mad, completely exhausted, I went up to my room and sank into an easy chair, incapable of thought, too weak to move. I was nothing but a suffering, vibrating machine, a thing that had been flayed alive; my soul was like an open wound.

"My old valet, Prosper, who had helped to lay Juliette in her coffin, and dress her for her last sleep, silently entered the room and asked:

" 'Will Monsieur have something?'

"I shook my head.

" 'Monsieur is wrong. Something will happen to Monsieur if he does not take care. Will Monsieur allow me to put him to bed?'

"I answered: 'No, leave me alone,' and he retired.

"The hours slipped by unperceived. Oh! What a terrible night! It was cold, the fire had died out in the huge grate, and the wind, the winter wind, frozen and laden with ice, beat against the windowpanes with a fiendish regularity.

"The hours slipped by unperceived. There I was, unable to sleep, broken, crushed, with eyes wide open, legs outstretched, body limp and inanimate, and my mind stupefied. Suddenly the big front door bell rang. The start I gave made the chair creak under me. The solemn, heavy sound rang through the empty building as through a vault. I turned round to see what time it was and found it was two o'clock. Who could possibly be coming at that time?

"Impatiently the bell rang again twice. No doubt the servants were afraid to get up. I took a candle, went downstairs and was going to ask: 'Who's there?' but felt ashamed of such weakness and slowly drew the heavy bolts. My heart was beating rapidly; I was afraid. I opened the door abruptly and distinguished a white figure standing in the darkness, rather like a phantom.

"I drew back, paralyzed with anguish, stammering:

" 'Who—who—who are you?'

"A voice replied: 'It is I, Father.'

"It was my daughter.

"I really thought I must be mad, and I retreated backward before the advancing specter. I moved away, making a sign with my hand as if to drive the phantom away, that peculiar gesture which you have already noticed and which I have never got rid of.

"'Don't be frightened, Father; I was not dead,' the apparition said. 'Somebody tried to steal my rings and cut off one of my fingers; the blood began to flow and that brought me to life again.' And then I saw that she was covered with blood.

"I fell on my knees, choking with sobs and panting for breath.

"When I had regained a little self-control, though I was still too distraught to realize the terrible happiness that had befallen me, I made her go up to my room, put her in the easy chair, and pulled the bell violently for Prosper to light the fire, get something to drink, and summon assistance.

"The man entered, stared at my daughter, gasped with alarm and horror, and dropped dead on the ground.

"It was he who had opened the vault, who had mutilated and then left my child, unable to destroy the traces of his theft. He had not even taken the trouble to replace the coffin in its niche, feeling quite convinced that I would not suspect him in whom I trusted absolutely.

"You see, sir, what an unhappy couple we are."

He was silent. Night had fallen, enveloping the little desolate mournful valley in its gloom, and a kind of mysterious dread came over me at being in the company of these strange beings: the dead returned from the grave, and the father with his alarming gestures.

What could I say? I murmured:

"What a horrible thing!"

Then, after a moment's silence, I added: "Let us go back. I think it's rather cold." And we returned to the hotel.

Thus I Refute Beelzy

by John Collier

Oh, the games that children play!

"There goes the tea bell," said Mrs. Carter. "I hope Simon hears it."

They looked out from the window of the drawing room. The long garden, agreeably neglected, ended in a waste plot. Here a little summerhouse was passing close by beauty on its way to complete decay. This was Simon's retreat. It was almost completely screened by the tangled branches of the apple tree and the pear tree, planted too close together, as they always are in suburban gardens. They caught a glimpse of him now and then, as he strutted up and down, mouthing and gesticulating, performing all the solemn mumbo jumbo of small boys who spend long afternoons at the forgotten ends of long gardens.

"There he is, bless him," said Betty.

"Playing his game," said Mrs. Carter. "He won't play with the other children anymore. And if I go down there—the temper! And comes in tired out."

"He doesn't have his sleep in the afternoons?" asked Betty.

"You know what Big Simon's ideas are," said Mrs. Carter. " 'Let him choose for himself,' he says. That's what he chooses, and he comes in as white as a sheet."

"Look. He's heard the bell," said Betty. The expression was justified, though the bell had ceased ringing a full minute ago. Small Simon stopped in his parade exactly as if its tinny dingle had at that moment reached his ear. They watched him perform certain ritual sweeps and scratchings with his little stick, and come lagging over the hot and flaggy grass towards the house.

Mrs. Carter led the way down to the playroom, or garden-room, which was also the tearoom for hot days. It had been the huge scullery of this tall Georgian house. Now the walls were cream-washed, there was coarse blue net in the windows, canvas-covered armchairs on the stone floor, and a reproduction of Van Gogh's *Sunflowers* over the mantelpiece.

Small Simon came drifting in, and accorded Betty a perfunctory greeting. His face was an almost perfect triangle, pointed at the chin, and he was paler than he should have been. "The little elf-child!" cried Betty.

Simon looked at her. "No," said he.

At that moment the door opened, and Mr. Carter came in, rubbing his hands. He was a dentist, and washed them before and after everything he did. "You!" said his wife. "Home already!"

"Not unwelcome, I hope," said Mr. Carter, nodding to Betty. "Two people canceled their appointments; I decided to come home. I said, I hope I am not unwelcome."

"Silly!" said his wife. "Of course not."

"Small Simon seems doubtful," continued Mr. Carter.

"Small Simon, are you sorry to see me at tea with you?"
"No, Daddy."
"No, what?"
"No, Big Simon."
"That's right. Big Simon and Small Simon. That sounds more like friends, doesn't it? At one time little boys had to call their father 'sir.' If they forgot—a good spanking. On the bottom, Small Simon! On the bottom!" said Mr. Carter, washing his hands once more with his invisible soap and water.

The little boy turned crimson with shame or rage.

"But now, you see," said Betty, to help, "you can call your father whatever you like."

"And what," asked Mr. Carter, "has Small Simon been doing this afternoon? While Big Simon has been at work."

"Nothing," muttered his son.

"Then you have been bored," said Mr. Carter. "Learn from experience, Small Simon. Tomorrow, do something amusing, and you will not be bored. I want him to learn from experience, Betty. That is my way, the new way."

"I have learned," said the boy, speaking like an old, tired man, as little boys so often do.

"It would hardly seem so," said Mr. Carter, "if you sit on your behind all the afternoon, doing nothing. Had *my* father caught me doing nothing, I should not have sat very comfortably."

"He played," said Mrs. Carter.

"A bit," said the boy, shifting on his chair.

"Too much," said Mrs. Carter. "He comes in all nervy and dazed. He ought to have his rest."

"He is six," said her husband. "He is a reasonable

being. He must choose for himself. But what game is this, Small Simon, that is worth getting nervy and dazed over? There are very few games as good as all that."

"It's nothing," said the boy.

"Oh, come," said his father. "We are friends, are we not? You can tell me. I was a Small Simon once, just like you, and played the same games you play. Of course there were no airplanes in those days. With whom do you play this fine game? Come on, we must all answer civil questions, or the world would never go round. With whom do you play?"

"Mr. Beelzy," said the boy, unable to resist.

"Mr. Beelzy?" said his father, raising his eyebrows inquiringly at his wife.

"It's a game he makes up," said she.

"Not makes up!" cried the boy. "Fool!"

"That is telling stories," said his mother. "And rude as well. We had better talk of something different."

"No wonder he is rude," said Mr. Carter, "if you say he tells lies, and then insist on changing the subject. He tells you his fantasy: you implant a guilt feeling. What can you expect? A defense mechanism. Then you get a real lie."

"Like in *These Three*," said Betty. "Only different, of course. *She* was an unblushing little liar."

"I would have made her blush," said Mr. Carter, "in the proper part of her anatomy. But Small Simon is in the fantasy stage. Are you not, Small Simon? You just make things up."

"No, I don't," said the boy.

"You do," said his father. "And because you do, it is not too late to reason with you. There is no harm in a fantasy, old chap. There is no harm in a bit of make-

Thus I Refute Beelzy

believe. Only you have to know the difference between daydreams and real things, or your brain will never grow. It will never be the brain of a Big Simon. So come on. Let us hear about this Mr. Beelzy of yours. Come on. What is he like?"

"He isn't like anything," said the boy.

"Like nothing on earth?" said his father. "That's a terrible fellow."

"I'm not frightened of him," said the child, smiling. "Not a bit."

"I should hope not," said his father. "If you were, you would be frightening yourself. I am always telling people, older people than you are, that they are just frightening themselves. Is he a funny man? Is he a giant?"

"Sometimes he is," said the little boy.

"Sometimes one thing, sometimes another," said his father. "Sounds pretty vague. Why can't you tell us just what he's like?"

"I love him," said the small boy. "He loves me."

"That's a big word," said Mr. Carter. "That might be better kept for real things, like Big Simon and Small Simon."

"He is real," said the boy, passionately. "He's not a fool. He's real."

"Listen," said his father. "When you go down the garden there's nobody there. Is there?"

"No," said the boy.

"Then you think of him, inside your head, and he comes."

"No," said Small Simon. "I have to do something with my stick."

"That doesn't matter."

"Yes, it does."

"Small Simon, you are being obstinate," said Mr. Carter. "I am trying to explain something to you. I have been longer in the world than you have, so naturally I am older and wiser. I am explaining that Mr. Beelzy is a fantasy of yours. Do you hear? Do you understand?"

"Yes, Daddy."

"He is a game. He is a let's-pretend."

The little boy looked down at his plate, smiling resignedly.

"I hope you are listening to me," said his father. "All you have to do is to say, 'I have been playing a game of let's-pretend. With someone I make up, called Mr. Beelzy.' Then no one will say you tell lies, and you will know the difference between dreams and reality. Mr. Beelzy is a daydream."

The little boy still stared at his plate.

"He is sometimes there and sometimes not there," pursued Mr. Carter. "Sometimes he's like one thing, sometimes another. You can't really see him. Not as you see me. I am real. You can't touch him. You can touch me. I can touch you." Mr. Carter stretched out his big, white, dentist's hand, and took his little son by the shoulder. He stopped speaking for a moment and tightened his hand. The little boy sank his head still lower.

"Now you know the difference," said Mr. Carter, "between a pretend and a real thing. You and I are one thing; he is another. Which is the pretend? Come on. Answer me. Which is the pretend?"

"Big Simon and Small Simon," said the little boy.

"Don't!" cried Betty, and at once put her hand over her mouth, for why should a visitor cry "Don't!" when a father is explaining things in a scientific and modern way?

"Well, my boy," said Mr. Carter, "I have said you must be allowed to learn from experience. Go upstairs. Right up to your room. You shall learn whether it is better to reason, or to be perverse and obstinate. Go up. I shall follow you."

"You are not going to beat the child?" cried Mrs. Carter.

"No," said the little boy. "Mr. Beelzy won't let him."

"Go on up with you!" shouted his father.

Small Simon stopped at the door. "He said he wouldn't let anyone hurt me," he whimpered. "He said he'd come like a lion, with wings on, and eat them up."

"You'll learn how real he is!" shouted his father after him. "If you can't learn it at one end, you shall learn it at the other. I'll have your breeches down. I shall finish my cup of tea first, however," said he to the two women.

Neither of them spoke. Mr. Carter finished his tea, and unhurriedly left the room, washing his hands with his invisible soap and water.

Mrs. Carter said nothing. Betty could think of nothing to say. She wanted to be talking: she was afraid of what they might hear.

Suddenly it came. It seemed to tear the air apart. "Good God!" she cried. "What was that? He's hurt him." She sprang out of her chair, her silly eyes flashing behind her glasses. "I'm going up there!" she cried, trembling.

"Yes, let us go up," said Mrs. Carter. "Let us go up. That was not Small Simon."

It was on the second-floor landing that they found the shoe, with the man's foot still in it, like that last morsel of a mouse which sometimes falls from the jaws of a hasty cat.

Keeping His Promise

by Algernon Blackwood

"The breathing was close beside him, almost on his cheek, and between him and the wall!"

It was eleven o'clock at night, and young Marriott was locked into his room, cramming as hard as he could cram. He was a "Fourth-Year Man" at Edinburgh University and he had been ploughed for this particular examination so often that his parents had positively declared they could no longer supply the funds to keep him there.

His rooms were cheap and dingy, but it was the lecture fees that took the money. So Marriott pulled himself together at last and definitely made up his mind that he would pass, or die in the attempt, and for some weeks now he had been reading as hard as mortal man can read. He was trying to make up for lost time and money in a way that showed conclusively he did not understand the value of either. For no ordinary man—and Marriott was in every sense an ordinary man—can afford to drive the mind as he had lately been driving his, without sooner or later paying the cost.

Among the students he had few friends or acquaintances, and these few had promised not to disturb him at night, knowing he was at last reading in earnest. It was, therefore, with feelings a good deal stronger than mere surprise that he heard his doorbell ring on this particular night and realized that he was to have a visitor. Some men would simply have muffled the bell and gone on quietly with their work. But Marriott was not this sort. He was nervous. It would have bothered and pecked at his mind all night long not to know who the visitor was and what he wanted. The only thing to do, therefore, was to let him in—and out again—as quickly as possible.

The landlady went to bed at ten o'clock punctually, after which hour nothing would induce her to pretend she heard the bell, so Marriott jumped up from his books with an exclamation that augured ill for the reception of his caller, and prepared to let him in with his own hand.

The streets of Edinburgh town were very still at this late hour—it was late for Edinburgh—and in the quiet neighborhood of F—— Street, where Marriott lived on the third floor, scarcely a sound broke the silence. As he crossed the floor, the bell rang a second time, with unnecessary clamor, and he unlocked the door and passed into the little hallway with considerable wrath and annoyance in his heart at the insolence of the double interruption.

"The fellows all know I'm reading for this exam. Why in the world do they come to bother me at such an unearthly hour?"

The inhabitants of the building, with himself, were medical students, general students, poor Writers to the

Signet, and some others whose vocations were perhaps not so obvious. The stone staircase, dimly lighted at each floor by a gas jet that would not turn above a certain height, wound down to the level of the street with no pretense at carpet or railing. At some levels it was cleaner than at others. It depended on the landlady of the particular level.

The acoustic properties of a spiral staircase seem to be peculiar. Marriott, standing by the open door, book in hand, thought every moment the owner of the footsteps would come into view. The sound of the boots was so close and so loud that they seemed to travel disproportionately in advance of their cause. Wondering who it could be, he stood ready with all manner of sharp greetings for the man who dared thus to disturb his work. But the man did not appear. The steps sounded almost under his nose, yet no one was visible.

A sudden queer sensation of fear passed over him — a faintness and a shiver down the back. It went, however, almost as soon as it came, and he was just debating whether he would call aloud to his invisible visitor, or slam the door and return to his books, when the cause of the disturbance turned the corner very slowly and came into view.

It was a stranger. He saw a youngish man, short of figure and very broad. His face was the color of a piece of chalk, and the eyes, which were very bright, had heavy lines underneath them. Though the cheeks and chin were unshaven and the general appearance unkempt, the man was evidently a gentleman, for he was well dressed and bore himself with a certain air. But, strangest of all, he wore no hat, and carried none in his hand, and although rain had been falling steadily all the evening, he appeared to have neither overcoat nor umbrella.

A hundred questions sprang up in Marriott's mind and rushed to his lips, chief among which was something like "Who in the world are you?" and "What in the name of Heaven do you come to me for?" But none of these questions found time to express themselves in words, for almost at once the caller turned his head a little so that the gaslight in the hall fell upon his features from a new angle. Then in a flash Marriott recognized him.

"Field! Man alive! Is it you?" he gasped.

The Fourth-Year Man was not lacking in intuition, and he perceived at once that here was a case for delicate treatment. He divined, without any actual process of thought, that the catastrophe often predicted had come at last, and that this man's father had turned him out of the house. They had been at a private school together years before, and though they had hardly met once since, the news had not failed to reach him from time to time with considerable detail, for the family lived near his own, and between certain of the sisters there was great intimacy. Young Field had gone wild later, he remembered hearing about it all—drink, a woman, opium, or something of the sort—he could not exactly call to mind.

"Come in," he said at once, his anger vanishing. "There's been something wrong, I can see. Come in, and tell me all about it and perhaps I can help—" He hardly knew what to say, and stammered a lot more besides. The dark side of life, and the horror of it, be longed to a world that lay remote from his own select little atmosphere of books and dreamings. But he had a man's heart for all that.

He led the way across the hall, shutting the front door carefully behind him, and noticed as he did so that the other, though certainly sober, was unsteady on his legs, and evidently much exhausted. Marriott might not be able to pass his examinations, but he at least knew the symptoms of starvation—acute starvation, unless he was much mistaken—when they stared him in the face.

"Come along," he said cheerfully, and with genuine sympathy in his voice. "I'm glad to see you. I was going to have a bite of something to eat, and you're just in time to join me."

The other made no audible reply, and shuffled so feebly with his feet that Marriott took his arm by way of support. He noticed for the first time that the clothes hung on him with pitiful looseness. The broad frame was literally hardly more than a frame. He was as thin as a skeleton. But, as he touched him, the sensation of faintness and dread returned. It only lasted a moment, and then passed off, and he ascribed it not unnaturally to the distress and shock of seeing a former friend in such a pitiful plight.

"Better let me guide you. It's shamefully dark—this hall. I'm always complaining," he said lightly, recognizing by the weight upon his arm that the guidance was sorely needed, "but the old cat never does anything except promise." He led him to the sofa, wondering all the time where he had come from and how he had found out the address. It must be at least seven years since those days at the private school when they used to be such close friends.

"Now, if you'll forgive me for a minute," he said, "I'll get supper ready—such as it is. And don't bother to talk. Just take it easy on the sofa. I see you're dead tired. You can tell me about it afterwards, and we'll make plans."

The other sat down on the edge of the sofa and stared in silence, while Marriott got out the brown loaf, scones, and a huge pot of marmalade that Edinburgh students always keep in their cupboards. His eyes shone with a brightness that suggested drugs, Marriott thought, stealing a glance at him from behind the cupboard door. He did not like yet to take a full square look. The fellow was in a bad way, and it would have been so like an examination to stare and wait for explanations. Besides, he was evidently almost too exhausted to speak. So, for reasons of delicacy—and for another reason as well which he could not exactly formulate to himself—he let his visitor rest apparently unnoticed, while he busied himself with the supper. He lit the spirit lamp to make cocoa, and when the water was boiling he drew up the table with the good things to the sofa, so that Field need not have even the trouble of moving to a chair.

"Now, let's tuck in," he said, "and afterwards we'll have a pipe and a chat. I'm reading for an exam, you know, and I always have something about this time. It's jolly to have a companion."

He looked up and caught his guest's eyes directed straight upon his own. An involuntary shudder ran through him from head to foot. The face opposite him was deadly white and wore a dreadful expression of pain and mental suffering.

"By Gad!" he said, jumping up, "I quite forgot. I've got some whiskey somewhere. What an ass I am. I never touch it myself when I'm working like this."

He went to the cupboard and poured out a stiff glass which the other swallowed at a single gulp, and without any water. Marriott watched him while he drank it, and at the same time noticed something else as well—Field's coat was all over dusty, and on one shoulder was a bit of cobweb. It was perfectly dry; Field arrived on a soaking wet night without hat, umbrella, or overcoat, and yet perfectly dry, even dusty. Therefore he had been under cover. What did it all mean? Had he been hiding in the building? . . .

It was very strange. Yet he volunteered nothing; and Marriott had pretty well made up his mind by this time that he would not ask any questions until he had eaten and slept. Food and sleep were obviously what the poor devil needed most and first—he was pleased with his powers of ready diagnosis—and it would not be fair to press him till he had recovered a bit.

They ate their supper together while the host carried on a running one-sided conversation, chiefly about himself and his exams and his "old cat" of a landlady, so that the guest need not utter a single word unless he really wished to—which he evidently did not! But, while he toyed with his food, feeling no desire to eat, the other ate voraciously. To see a hungry man devour cold scones, stale oatcake, and brown bread laden with marmalade was a revelation to this inexperienced student who had never known what it was to be without at least three meals a day. He watched in spite of himself, wondering why the fellow did not choke in the process. But Field seemed to be as sleepy as he was hungry. More than once his head dropped and he ceased to masticate the food in his mouth. Marriott had positively to shake him before he would go on with his meal. A stronger emotion will overcome a weaker, but this struggle between the sting of real hunger and the magical opiate of overpowering sleep was a curious sight to the student, who watched it with mingled astonishment and alarm. He had heard of the pleasure it was to feed hungry men, and watch them eat, but he had never actually witnessed it, and he had no idea it was like this. Field ate like an animal—gobbled, stuffed, gorged. Marriott forgot his reading, and began to feel something very much like a lump in his throat.

"Afraid there's been awfully little to offer you, old man," he managed to blurt out when at length the last scone had disappeared, and the rapid, one-sided meal was at an end. Field still made no reply, for he was almost asleep in his seat. He merely looked up wearily and gratefully.

"Now you must have some sleep, you know," he continued, "or you'll go to pieces. I shall be up all night reading for this blessed exam. You're more than welcome to my bed. Tomorrow we'll have a late breakfast and—and see what can be done—and make plans—I'm awfully good at making plans, you know," he added with an attempt at lightness.

Field maintained his "dead sleepy" silence, but appeared to acquiesce, and the other led the way into the bedroom, apologizing as he did so to this half-starved son of a baronet—whose own home was almost a palace—for the size of the room. The weary guest, however, made no pretense of thanks or politeness. He merely steadied himself on his friend's arm as he staggered across the room, and then, with all his clothes on, dropped his exhausted body on the bed. In less than a minute he was to all appearances sound asleep.

For several minutes Marriott stood in the open door and watched him; praying devoutly that he might never find himself in a like predicament, and then fell to wondering what he would do with his unbidden guest on the morrow. But he did not stop long to think, for the call of his books was imperative, and happen what might, he must see to it that he passed that examination.

Having again locked the door into the hall, he sat down to his books and resumed his notes on *materia medica* where he had left off when the bell rang. But it was difficult for some time to concentrate his mind on the subject. His thoughts kept wandering to the picture of that white-faced, strange-eyed fellow, starved and dirty, lying in his clothes and boots on the bed. He recalled their schooldays together before they had drifted apart, and how they had vowed eternal friendship—and all the rest of it. And now! What horrible straits to be in. How could any man let the love of dissipation take such hold upon him?

But one of their vows together Marriott, it seemed, had completely forgotten. Just now, at any rate, it lay too far in the background of his memory to be recalled.

Through the half-open door—the bedroom led out of the sitting room and had no other door—came the sound of deep, long-drawn breathing, the regular steady breathing of a tired man, so tired that, even to listen to it made Marriott almost want to go to sleep himself.

"He needed it," reflected the student, "and perhaps it came only just in time!"

Perhaps so; for outside the bitter wind from across the Forth howled cruelly and drove the rain in cold streams against the windowpanes, and down the deserted streets. Long before Marriott settled down again properly to his reading, he heard distinctly, as it were, through the sentences of the book, the heavy, deep breathing of the sleeper in the next room.

A couple of hours later, when he yawned and changed his books, he still heard the breathing, and went cautiously up to the door to look round.

At first the darkness of the room must have deceived him, or else his eyes were confused and dazzled by the recent glare of the reading lamp. For a minute or two he could make out nothing at all but dark lumps of furniture, the mass of the chest of drawers by the wall, and the white patch where his bath stood in the center of the floor.

Then the bed came slowly into view. And on it he saw the outline of the sleeping body gradually take shape before his eyes, growing up strangely into the darkness, till it stood out in marked relief—the long black form against the white counterpane.

He could hardly help smiling. Field had not moved an inch. He watched him a moment or two and then returned to his books. The night was full of the singing voices of the wind and rain. There was no sound of traffic; no hansoms clattered over the cobbles, and it was still too early for the milk carts. He worked on steadily and conscientiously, only stopping now and again to change a book, or to sip some of the poisonous stuff that kept him awake and made his brain so active, and on these occasions Field's breathing was always distinctly audible in the room. Outside, the storm continued to howl, but inside the house all was stillness. The shade of the reading lamp threw all the light upon the littered table, leaving the other end of the room in comparative darkness. The bedroom door was exactly opposite him where he sat. There was nothing to disturb the worker, nothing but an occasional rush of wind against the windows, and a slight pain in his arm.

This pain, however, which he was unable to account for, grew once or twice very acute. It bothered him; and he tried to remember how, and when, he could have bruised himself so severely, but without success.

At length the page before him turned from yellow to gray, and there were sounds of wheels in the street below. It was four o'clock. Marriott leaned back and yawned prodigiously. Then he drew back the curtains. The storm had subsided and the Castle Rock was shrouded in mist. With another yawn he turned away from the dreary outlook and prepared to sleep the remaining four hours till breakfast on the sofa. Field was still breathing heavily in the next room, and he first tiptoed across the floor to take another look at him.

Peering cautiously round the half-opened door his first glance fell upon the bed now plainly discernible in the gray light of morning. He stared hard. Then he rubbed his eyes. Then he rubbed his eyes again and thrust his head farther round the edge of the door. With fixed eyes, he stared harder still, and harder.

But it made no difference at all. He was staring into an empty room.

The sensation of fear he had felt when Field first appeared upon the scene returned suddenly, but with much greater force. He became conscious, too, that his left arm was throbbing violently and causing him great pain. He stood wondering, and staring, and trying to collect his thoughts. He was trembling from head to foot.

By a great effort of the will he left the support of the door and walked forward boldly into the room.

There, upon the bed, was the impress of a body, where Field had lain and slept. There was the mark of the head on the pillow, and the slight indentation at the foot of the bed where the boots had rested on the counterpane. And there, plainer than ever—for he was closer to it—was *the breathing*!

Marriott tried to pull himself together. With a great effort he found his voice and called his friend aloud by name!

"Field! Is that you? Where are you?"

There was no reply; but the breathing continued without interruption, coming directly from the bed. His voice had such an unfamiliar sound that Marriott did not care to repeat his questions, but he went down on his knees and examined the bed above and below, pulling the mattress off finally, and taking the coverings away separately one by one. But though the sounds continued, there was no visible sign of Field, nor was there any space in which a human being, however small, could have concealed itself. He pulled the bed out from the wall, but the sound *stayed where it was*. It did not move with the bed.

Marriott, finding self-control a little difficult in his weary condition, at once set about a thorough search of the room. He went through the cupboard, the chest of drawers, the little alcove where the clothes hung—

everything. But there was no sign of anyone. The small window near the ceiling was closed; and, anyhow, was not large enough to let a cat pass. The sitting-room door was locked on the inside; he could not have got out that way. Curious thoughts began to trouble Marriott's mind, bringing in their train unwelcome sensations. He grew more and more excited; he searched the bed again till it resembled the scene of a pillow fight; he searched both rooms, knowing all the time it was useless—and then he searched again. A cold perspiration broke out all over his body; and the sound of heavy breathing, all this time, never ceased to come from the corner where Field had lain down to sleep.

Then he tried something else. He pushed the bed back exactly into its original position—and himself lay down upon it just where his guest had lain. But the same instant he sprang up again in a single bound. The breathing was close beside him, almost on his cheek, and between him and the wall! Not even a child could have squeezed into the space.

He went back into his sitting-room, opened the windows, welcoming all the light and air possible, and tried to think the whole matter over quietly and clearly. Men who read too hard, and slept too little, he knew were sometimes troubled with very vivid hallucinations. Again he calmly reviewed every incident of the night: his accurate sensations; the vivid details; the emotions stirred in him; the dreadful feast—no single hallucination could ever combine all these and cover so long a period of time. But with less satisfaction he thought of the recurring faintness, and curious sense of horror that had once or twice come over him, and then of the violent pains in his arm. These were quite unaccountable.

Moreover, now that he began to analyze and examine, there was one other thing that fell upon him like a sudden revelation: *During the whole time Field had not actually uttered a single word!* Yet, as though in mockery upon his reflections, there came ever from that inner room the sound of the breathing, long-drawn, deep, and regular. The thing was incredible. It was absurd.

Haunted by visions of brain fever and insanity, Marriott put on his cap and mackintosh and left the house. The morning air on Arthur's Seat would blow the cobwebs from his brain; the scent of the heather, and above all, the sight of the sea. He roamed over the wet slopes above Holyrood for a couple of hours, and did not return until the exercise had shaken some of the horror out of his bones, and given him a ravening appetite into the bargain.

As he entered he saw that there was another man in the room, standing against the window with his back to the light. He recognized his fellow student, Greene, who was reading for the same examination.

"Read hard all night, Marriott," he said, "and thought I'd drop in here to compare notes and have some breakfast. You're out early?" he added, by way of a question. Marriott said he had a headache and a walk had helped it, and Greene nodded and said, "Ah!" But when the girl had set the steaming porridge on the table and gone out again, he went on with rather a forced tone, "Didn't know you had any friends who drank, Marriott?"

This was obviously tentative, and Marriott replied dryly that he did not know it either.

"Sounds just as if some chap were 'sleeping it off' in there, doesn't it, though?" persisted the other, with a nod in the direction of the bedroom, and looking curiously at his friend. The two men stared steadily at each other for several seconds, and then Marriott said earnestly:

"Then you hear it too, thank God!"

"Of course I hear it. The door's open. Sorry if I wasn't meant to."

"Oh, I don't mean that," said Marriott, lowering his voice. "But I'm awfully relieved. Let me explain. Of course, if you hear it too, then it's all right; but really it frightened me more than I can tell you. I thought I was going to have brain fever, or something, and you know what a lot depends on this exam. It always begins with sounds, or visions, or some sort of beastly hallucination, and I—"

"Rot!" ejaculated the other impatiently. "What *are* you talking about?"

"Now, listen to me, Greene," said Marriott, as calmly as he could, for the breathing was still plainly audible, "and I'll tell you what I mean, only don't interrupt." And thereupon he related exactly what had happened during the night, telling everything, even down to the pain in his arm. When it was over he got up from the table and crossed the room.

"You hear the breathing now plainly, don't you?" he said. Greene said he did. "Well, come with me, and we'll search the room together." The other, however, did not move from his chair.

"I've been in already," he said sheepishly; "I heard the sounds and thought it was you. The door was ajar —so I went in."

Marriott made no comment, but pushed the door

open as wide as it would go. As it opened, the sound of breathing grew more and more distinct.

"*Someone* must be in there," said Greene under his breath.

"*Someone* is in there, but *where?*" said Marriott. Again he urged his friend to go in with him. But Greene refused point-blank; said he had been in once and had searched the room and there was nothing there. He would not go in again for a good deal.

They shut the door and retired into the other room to talk it all over with many pipes. Greene questioned his friend very closely, but without illuminating result, since questions cannot alter facts.

"The only thing that ought to have a proper, a logical explanation is the pain in my arm," said Marriott, rubbing that member with an attempt at a smile. "It hurts so infernally and aches all the way up. I can't remember bruising it, though."

"Let me examine it for you," said Greene. "I'm awfully good at bones in spite of the examiners' opinion to the contrary." It was a relief to play the fool a bit, and Marriott took his coat off and rolled up his sleeve.

"By George, though, I'm bleeding!" he exclaimed. "Look here! What on earth's this?"

On the forearm, quite close to the wrist, was a thin red line. There was a tiny drop of apparently fresh blood on it. Greene came over and looked closely at it for some minutes. Then he sat back in his chair, looking curiously at his friend's face.

"You've scratched yourself without knowing it," he said presently.

"There's no sign of a bruise. It must be something else that made my arm ache."

Marriott sat very still, staring silently at his arm as though the solution of the whole mystery lay there actually written upon the skin.

"What's the matter? I see nothing very strange about a scratch," said Greene, in an unconvincing sort of voice. "It was your cuff links probably. Last night in your excitement—"

But Marriott, white to the very lips, was trying to speak. The sweat stood in great beads on his forehead. At last he leaned forward close to his friend's face.

"Look," he said, in a low voice that shook a little. "Do you see that red mark? I mean *underneath* what you call the scratch?"

Greene admitted he saw something or other, and Marriott wiped the place clean with his handkerchief and told him to look again more closely.

"Yes, I see," returned the other, lifting his head after a moment's careful inspection. "It looks like an old scar."

"It *is* an old scar," whispered Marriott, his lips trembling. "*Now* it all comes back to me."

"All what?" Greene fidgeted on his chair. He tried to laugh, but without success. His friend seemed bordering on collapse.

"Hush! Be quiet, and—I'll tell you," he said. "*Field made that scar.*"

For a whole minute the two men looked each other full in the face without speaking.

"Field made that scar!" repeated Marriott at length in a louder voice.

"Field! You mean—last night?"

Keeping His Promise 43

"No, not last night. Years ago—at school, with his knife. And I made a scar in his arm with mine." Marriott was talking rapidly now.

"We exchanged drops of blood in each other's cuts. He put a drop into my arm and I put one into his—"

"In the name of Heaven, what for?"

"It was a boys' compact. We made a sacred pledge, a bargain. I remember it all perfectly now. We had been reading some dreadful book and we swore to appear to one another—I mean, whoever died first swore to show himself to the other. And we sealed the compact with each other's blood. I remember it all so well—the hot summer afternoon in the playground, seven years ago —and one of the masters caught us and confiscated the knives—and I have never thought of it again to this day—"

"And you mean—" stammered Greene.

But Marriott made no answer. He got up and crossed the room and lay down wearily upon the sofa, hiding his face in his hands.

Greene himself was a bit nonplussed. He left his friend alone for a little while, thinking it all over again. Suddenly an idea seemed to strike him. He went over to where Marriott still lay motionless on the sofa and roused him. In any case it was better to face the matter, whether there was an explanation or not. Giving in was always the silly exit.

"I say, Marriott," he began, as the other turned his white face up to him. "There's no good being so upset about it. I mean—if it's all a hallucination we know what to do. And if it isn't—well, we know what to think, don't we?"

"I suppose so. But it frightens me horribly for some

reason," returned his friend in a hushed voice. "And that poor devil—"

"But, after all, if the worst is true and—and that chap *has* kept his promise—well, he has, that's all, isn't it?"

Marriott nodded.

"There's only one thing that occurs to me," Greene went on, "and that is, are you quite sure that—that he really ate like that—I mean, that he actually *ate anything at all?*" he finished, blurting out all his thought.

Marriott stared at him for a moment and then said he could easily make certain. He spoke quietly. After the main shock no lesser surprise could affect him.

"I put the things away myself," he said, "after we had finished. They are on the third shelf in that cupboard. No one's touched 'em since."

He pointed without getting up, and Greene took the hint and went over to look.

"Exactly," he said, after a brief examination; "just as I thought. It was partly hallucination, at any rate. The things haven't been touched. Come and see for yourself."

Together they examined the shelf. There was the brown loaf, the plate of stale scones, the oatcake, all untouched. Even the glass of whiskey Marriott had poured out stood there with the whiskey still in it.

"You were feeding—no one," said Greene. "Field ate and drank nothing. He was not there at all!"

"But the breathing?" urged the other in a low voice, staring with a dazed expression on his face.

Greene did not answer. He walked over to the bedroom, while Marriott followed him with his eyes. He opened the door, and listened. There was no need for words. The sound of deep, regular breathing came floating through the air. There was no hallucination about that, at any rate. Marriott could hear it where he stood on the other side of the room.

Greene closed the door and came back. "There's only one thing to do," he declared with decision. "Write home and find out about him, and meanwhile come and finish your reading in my rooms. I've got an extra bed."

"Agreed," returned the Fourth-Year Man; "there's no hallucination about that exam; I must pass that whatever happens."

And this was what they did.

It was about a week later when Marriott got the answer from his sister. Part of it he read out to Greene:

"It is curious," she wrote, "that in your letter you should have inquired after Field. It seems a terrible thing, but you know only a short while ago Sir John's patience became exhausted, and he turned him out of the house, they say without a penny. Well, what do you think? He has killed himself. At least, it looks like suicide. Instead of leaving the house, he went down into the cellar and simply starved himself to death. . . . They're trying to suppress it, of course, but I heard it all from my maid, who got it from their footman. . . . They found the body on the fourteenth, and the doctor said he had died about twelve hours before. . . . He was dreadfully thin. . . ."

"Then he died on the thirteenth," said Greene.

Marriott nodded.

"That's the very night he came to see you."

Marriott nodded again.

The House

by André Maurois

TRANSLATED BY ADRIENNE FOULKE

"'Haunted?' I said. 'That
will scarcely stop me.'"

"Two years ago," she said, "when I was so sick, I realized that I was dreaming the same dream night after night. I was walking in the country. In the distance, I could see a white house, low and long, that was surrounded by a grove of linden trees. To the left of the house, a meadow bordered by poplars pleasantly interrupted the symmetry of the scene, and the tips of the poplars, which you could see from far off, were swaying above the linden.

"In my dream, I was was drawn to this house, and I walked toward it. A white wooden gate closed the entrance. I opened it and walked along a gracefully curving path. The path was lined by trees, and under the trees I found spring flowers—primroses and periwinkles and anemones that faded the moment I picked them. As I came to the end of this path, I was only a few steps from the house. In front of the house, there was

The House

a great green expanse, clipped like the English lawns. It was bare, except for a single bed of violet flowers encircling it.

"The house was built of white stone and it had a slate roof. The door—a light-oak door with carved panels—was at the top of a flight of steps. I wanted to visit the house, but no one answered when I called. I was terribly disappointed, and I rang and I shouted—and finally I woke up.

"That was my dream, and for months it kept coming back with such precision and fidelity that finally I thought: Surely I must have seen this park and this house as a child. When I would wake up, however, I could never recapture it in waking memory. The search for it became such an obsession that one summer—I'd learned to drive a little car—I decided to spend my vacation driving through France in search of my dream house.

"I'm not going to tell you about my travels. I explored Normandy, Touraine, Poitou, and found nothing, which didn't surprise me. In October, I came back to Paris, and all through the winter I continued to dream about the white house. Last spring, I resumed my old habit of making excursions in the outskirts of Paris. One day, I was crossing a valley near l'Isle-Adam. Suddenly I felt an agreeable shock—that strange feeling one has when after a long absence one recognizes people or places one has loved.

"Although I had never been in that particular area before, I was perfectly familiar with the landscape lying to my right. The crests of some poplars dominated a stand of linden trees. Through the foliage, which was still sparse, I could glimpse a house. Then I knew that

I had found my dream château. I was quite aware that a hundred yards ahead, a narrow road would be cutting across the highway. The road was there. I followed it. It led me to a white gate.

"There began the path I had so often followed. Under the trees, I admired the carpet of soft colors woven by the periwinkles, the primroses, and the anemones. When I came to the end of the row of linden, I saw the green lawn and the little flight of steps, at the top of which was the light-oak door. I got out of my car, ran quickly up the steps, and rang the bell.

"I was terribly afraid that no one would answer, but almost immediately a servant appeared. It was a man, with a sad face, very old. He was wearing a black jacket. He seemed very much surprised to see me, and he looked at me closely without saying a word.

" 'I'm going to ask you a rather odd favor,' I said, 'I don't know the owners of this house, but I would be very happy if they would permit me to visit it.'

" 'The château is for rent, Madame,' he said, with what struck me as regret, 'and I am here to show it.'

" 'To rent?' I said. 'What luck! It's too much to have hoped for. But how is it that the owners of such a beautiful house aren't living in it?'

" 'The owners did live in it, Madame. They moved out when it became haunted.'

" 'Haunted?' I said. 'That will scarcely stop me. I didn't know people in France, even in the the country, still believed in ghosts.'

" 'I wouldn't believe in them, Madame,' he said seriously, 'if I myself had not met, in the park at night, the phantom that drove my employers away.'

"'What a story!' I said, trying to smile.

"'A story, Madame,' the old man said, with an air of reproach, 'that you least of all should laugh at, since the phantom was you.'"

The Call of the Hand

by Louis Golding

Alas, the brothers were inseparable.

I

No one knew what sin Nikolai Kupreloff had committed to bring on his head so terrible a penalty. Year after year his wife and he had prayed for a child, to their icons in the tiny basilica in the wood, and when his wife gave birth at last, it was neither a child nor children. She had given birth to two little boys, perfectly made, exquisitely proportioned, but there was a deadly thing had befallen them . . . the tiny right hand of the one was inexorably seized by the left hand of the other.

The little woodcutter's cottage of Nikolai lay deeply hidden in the great pine woods of Lower Serbia, miles from his nearest neighbor. Yet even in that wild country the fame of the intertwined children traveled far, and the wise old women from those parts came to see if herbs or chanting or any of their dark gifts might be of the least avail. They were no more useful than a real doctor who had studied at Belgrade, was practicing at

Monastir, and was stimulated to great interest by the account of these strange children. The case defied all the arts of black or white magic, and the interest of the episode flickered and died down.

So it was that Nikolai reconciled himself to the inevitable, and as the boys grew older he would cross himself devoutly and say, "Thank God, it might have been a thousand times worse!" They were lads of extraordinary beauty. Peter and Ivan he called them, Ivan being the lad who held so irrevocably the wrist of his brother within his fingers. In appearance they were identical—the light, tough hair and the laughing blue eyes of the Serbian Slav, sturdy, well-knit limbs, and a sterling robustness of physique. It was only their parents and themselves who knew that between them there was one slight but unmistakable mark of distinction— below the knuckle of Ivan's thumb was marked dully a little red arrow. In fact, a stranger might not have known that this abnormal bond existed between the two brothers as he saw them swinging along under the pines. "What a loving little pair!" he would exclaim, as he heard them laugh and chatter in complete harmony, and look into each other's eyes with the understanding born of flawless love.

When they were about fifteen years old their mother died, and the father Nikolai began more and more to remain behind in his cottage attending to the frugal needs of the little family, while Peter and Ivan, as the years went on, grew even more skillful in the art of woodcutting; for Peter wielding the axe in his left hand, Ivan in his right, achieved such a fine reciprocity of movement, that Nikolai would laugh in his great yellow beard and mutter, "Truly the ways of God are inscrutable, for even out of their calamity has He made a great blessing!" The passing of time only knit closer their perfect intimacy, so that they almost did not notice when their father Nikolai sickened and died. Now they were left to their cottage and their woodcutting and their complete love, the whole being crowned by the splendid physique of young foresters at twenty-one; so that life, it seemed, had nothing in store for them but long years of undivided love and content.

Yet even into their seclusion rumors came of the great world beyond. Now and again they would catch glimpses of the marvels of Salonika in the eyes of traveled men. They would hear of a city where lovely women, infinitely more beautiful than the queen of the tousled gypsies who flickered from time to time along the forest paths, sang upon stages of golden wood, in gardens full of hanging lights. They would hear of the sea and glowing ships, and men who spoke low musical languages uttered in countries beyond the sea.

So it was the brothers determined to leave their woodcutting behind them for a season and adventure forth into the world of ships and songs and lovely women.

2

To Peter and Ivan, Salonika was a revelation of wonders they barely thought actual. From a little room in the street of Johann Tschimiski they saw the multicolored tides of cosmopolitan humanity sweeping down from Egnatia Street, down Venizelos Street to the Place de la Concorde. They would walk along the quayside past the great hotels to the Jardins de la Tour Blanche, and were sent into an ecstasy of delight by the *chic* little women who smiled archly at these two fair-headed lads from the up-country, who walked along wrist clasped in hand in so naive and rustic a manner. Yet when they entered the Théatre des Variétés at the White Tower it seemed to them that the very portals of heaven had opened wide. They would return in a daze of delight to their room and recount with an almost religious fervor the beauties and enchantments of the show. Each little Spanish or French girl who came to do her song or minuet had seemed to them more enchanting than the last. Never a cloud of disagreement came between them. There was a perfect coincidence in their tastes, and never, they felt, had their love for each other been so sympathetic and complete as it was now.

The brothers had no large sum of money at their disposal. The time of their holiday was drawing to a close. One evening they turned up at the theater for the last time, their nerves keyed up to a pitch of delighted impatience, the more tense as the brothers knew that the next day would see them on the arduous road back to their Serbian forest. Turn followed turn with alluring consequence. Then at one stage the music ceased for some moments and there was an atmosphere of expectance in the air. It was then that a simple and delightful English girl came half-shyly from the wings. There was nothing flamboyant in her appearance or her manner. Yet at once she seemed to seize the house with the graceful and reticent winsomeness of her song. So she sang her song through, a dainty little ballad of old-world gardens and fragrant flowers and love unto death. Peter felt the fingers of Ivan tighten round his wrist. He himself had been so stirred to his depths by the gentle grace of the girl that it was with a slight feeling of resentment he realized that Ivan had been experiencing once again an identical emotion. As he involuntarily moved away his arm Ivan uttered a slight cry of impatience. He turned round and looked into Peter's eyes and found them aflame with a light deeper than mere appreciation. Peter was aware of his brother's glance and looked at Ivan in return to find his face flushed almost as if he were half-drunk.

That night for the first time in their history there occurred a slight bickering between the two. No mention of the little English actress passed between them, but each of them determined that some day, when his brother's interest had died away, he should broach the subject and the possibility of a rediscovery of the English actress at Salonika.

Next day they entrained for Monastir, and a few days later saw them installed once again in their father's cottage in the wood.

3

In proportion as the fortunes of the Kupreloff brothers increased, something that had once existed between them receded further away. The perfection of their old intimacy became a memory of the past. No longer did the most minute physical or spiritual experience of the one become automatically part of his brother's consciousness. So that now for the first time their indissoluble partnership became more and more galling.

There was no doubt of it. Everything dated from that last night at Salonika, when the English girl appeared on the stage. They would still occasionally revive something of the old fervor as they discussed from time to time their impressions of the unforgettable holiday. Yet

The Call of the Hand

never a word passed between them concerning the unconscious girl who had captured both their hearts. At night they would lie awake, each thinking that the other was asleep. Bitterly, definitely, they would confess to their own deep hearts, "She is mine, she is mine; I am hers for ever." And yet to each their love seemed hopeless beyond recall. There was the double sting that each of them loved the girl with an intensity reserved hitherto for his brother; but, if possible, more fatal was the despairing conviction that no girl could ever love the one of two brothers to whom the other would remain physically attached till death carried them both away. As the months passed by the friction between them increased. They were now in a position to buy land and a little livestock. But if Peter insisted upon keeping pigs, in the fashion of the majority of Serbians, Ivan would insist upon cattle. If Peter felt that he had done enough woodcutting for the day, Ivan felt that the day was only just beginning.

One night in late autumn Peter lay tossing very heavily in his sleep. Ivan lay awake, thinking, thinking for ever of the girl, his whole heart full of rancor against the brother who must for ever prevent the consummation of his love. Heavily, wearily, Peter heaved on the bed. Outside the wind was howling. The dreariness of the wind seemed to enter Peter's heart. "My little girl," he murmured, "my little girl! When shall we meet, my little girl? Never, never, never!" Ivan's forehead contracted with hate. He was filled suddenly with a tremendous loathing of his brother. "Never, never, never!" moaned Peter. Suddenly, obeying a frantic impulse, Ivan pulled with all his strength away from his brother's wrist to which Fate had so viciously fastened him. With a great scream of pain Peter half leapt from the bed.

"What's this? What do you mean?" he shouted, his voice thick with pain and sleep. "Nothing! Nothing! I couldn't help it! I was dreaming!" replied Ivan savagely, and the brothers settled down again for the night.

Night after night the same thing happened. Peter would murmur for ever in his sleep, "My little girl, when shall we meet? Never, never, never!" Ivan would lie awake, hatred surging violently through his whole body, till his eyes would see nothing but flames in the darkness of their log-built room; and the sound of the branches in the forest would begin to mutter and moan, "Have done with it, Ivan, have done with it! She is waiting for you, waiting, always waiting. Have done with it! Have done with *him*—with *him*—with *him*!"

One desolate night towards mid-winter the room was full of the miserable sleep-cries of Peter. Outside thunder ripped among the clouds. A finger of lightning came suddenly through the windows and pointed with a gesture of flame towards the open breast of Peter. A sudden and terrible thought flooded into Ivan's soul! Whatever there was of human kindness and brother-love seemed in one sinister moment to be washed away from before the onset of the flood. All the branches upon all the trees shrieked across the night. "We shall be quiet, you shall have rest. She shall be yours. Have done with him, have done with him!"

A great calm settled down upon Ivan's soul—the issue was decided, the issue which had been hovering for so long in his subconsciousness was decided at last. There was nothing left to do. The mere deed was the mere snapping of a thread. With his eyes wide open, a terrible

The Call of the Hand

silence lying upon his soul, he stared into the night, waiting, waiting for the dawn.

Dawn came at last. The brothers washed and took food. There was a long way to go, far off into the woods. There was almost a tenderness in Ivan's attitude towards Peter. What mattered now? The issue was decided; the gods had taken the thing out of his hands. With their axes swinging they made their way into the woods, through a day sharp with frost. At last they arrived at the clearing where they were to continue their tree-felling. A brazier stood waiting there, and before work started they lit a fire in preparation for the midday meal. Then they picked up their axes and set to. Lustily their strokes rang through the wood. Chime rang upon chime. It was strenuous work, the work of men with strong muscles and keen eyes.

The morning went by steadily. There was no hate in Ivan's soul—only a deadly patience. He knew the moment would come. He knew when the moment came that he would act. For a few minutes they stopped and wiped their foreheads. Peter opened his shirt wide and exposed his breast to Ivan. The quick vision presented itself of Peter heaving darkly in their bed, the sudden finger of lightning, the naked breast.

"Come!" said Ivan thickly, "let us begin!"

They both took up their positions against a tree. Peter with the axe in his left hand struck against the tree. Ivan, quick as the lightning which last night had shown him his way, whirled his axe round, away from the tree, and the sharp edge went cracking through Peter's ribs, deep beyond the heart. A great fountain of blood spurted into the air. A long, feeble moan left Peter's lips.

Deeper than the axe had cut, his eyes looked sorrowfully into the soul of Ivan. His weight tottered and Ivan felt himself following to the ground. There was not a moment to lose. Again the axe whirled through the air. With the whole of a strong man's strength the axe came down upon his own wrist, and down fell the body of Peter with the hand of his brother indissoluble in death round his wrist, as it had been indissoluble in life.

The thing he had brought about was too monstrous for Ivan at that moment to understand. It was only the little things that his ear and eye seized—the frightened screech of a bird in a tree, the sullen shining of the little red arrow in the thumb of his own severed hand.

Ivan felt the blood streaming from the stump of his forearm. He knew that if he did not reassert complete mastery over himself he would bleed to death. All would be vain—the call of the far girl, the murder, the last look in Peter's eyes. He staggered over to the brazier and plunged his forearm for one swift instant into the embers. Then darkness overwhelmed him and he fell backward into unutterable night.

4

It was easy enough to explain. Not the least suspicion attached itself to Ivan. People came from remote cabins and farms to sympathize with the bereaved brother. What was more likely in the world than that Ivan's axe should slide from a knot in the tree and come crashing against Peter, who, even if he could see the axe coming, could not by any human means have disengaged himself from his brother. "I always thought something like this would happen," people muttered wisely to each other, and shook their heads and crossed their breasts.

The Call of the Hand

Of course they all understood how Ivan could no longer remain in the cottage consecrated by memories of his brother. So Ivan sold his accumulation of timber and his land and what little stock the brothers had bought, and it was not many weeks after his forearm was healed that the jangling train from Monastir was bearing him through the Macedonian hills upon his quest for the English girl at Salonika.

In Salonika she was nowhere to be found. Forlornly he went from music hall to music hall, but she was gone. He haunted even the *cafés chantants* along Egnatia Street, even the degenerate *brasseries* on the Monastir Road, where the red-costumed women stood upon improvised platforms and sang to tipsy crowds with the accompaniment of feeble violins. But there was no trace of her in the whole city. From the director at the White Tower he learned that perhaps she had proceeded to Constantinople, perhaps she had returned to Athens, whence the European artistes generally came to Salonika on their round of the greater Levantine towns.

With all the fervor and idealism of a mediæval knight Ivan stepped upon the deck of a Messageries Maritimes boat returning to Marseilles by way of the Piraeus. When the electric train from the harbor landed him at the station in Athens a mystic conviction filled him that here in this city, some day, the English girl would be revealed to him. Ambitiously he first tried the great *Opéra*, but she was not there. The weeks lengthened into months and failure followed failure, but the mysterious foreknowledge of his race held up his weary spirits and bade him put aside despair.

When at last she appeared upon the stage of one of

the lesser music halls, it was with no great start of surprise or welcome that he recognized her arrival. It was as if a mother or a sister had slipped back into the place from which for some reason she had been absent. Her features had become engraved upon every curve of his brain. She came upon the stage and filled his life again as naturally as day fills the place of night. Life became for him a thing of meaning and splendor. He realized that at last Life was to begin.

He knew little of the half-measures and half-advances of Western civilization. He lost no time in appearing before the girl. After only a few words of difficult apology, with a voice of low and subdued passion he told her a fragment or two of his tale. It was a broken French that he talked—the French of which his mother long ago had taught her boys the few phrases she knew, and which his experiences in Salonika and Athens during the last few months had greatly improved.

The large gray eyes of the English girl opened wide in wonder as she listened, fascinated, to the stammering avowals of this tall stranger from a shadowy land. Half in fright she drew back against the wall of her wretched little dressing room, but, even so soon she realized that the destiny was overwhelming her which was to bring an end to her wanderings. She consented shyly to his suggestion that she should see him for a little while next night, and it was with a thrill of delight and fear she saw his great figure waiting for her at the gate of the Museum, as the purple Athenian dusk came wandering down from the Acropolis and cast velvet glooms among the pillars of Pentelican marble.

For years since her mother had died and her father had become a confirmed drunkard, it was a very lonely life that Mary Weston had led. She had no great talent, and she had drifted from theater to theater upon the Continent, for to her England was a place of no kindly memories. Ivan Kupreloff began to mean for her what her mother had meant before she died and her father before he had taken to drink.

A few months had passed only. There was no escape from Ivan. There was nothing importunate about him, but he was irresistible. He was Life. Proudly he realized that he had conquered her. To world's end and Time's end she was his own.

They were married at length. Athens and all the cities she had known, the Serbian wood and the murdered brother—these passed utterly from their souls in the strong kiss which united them for all days.

5

Yet not for ever was the memory of his dead life to vanish from the heart of Ivan. Even during the times of his most passionate love for Mary there began to invade him moments of bitter memory and regret. There was something which prevented the entire fusion with Mary towards which he yearned and ached. It was something deep in his soul. It was something which gnawed at his forearm, bit with teeth of contrition at the place where the axe had fallen and severed the hand from the wrist.

He tried to put all this futility from him. He would seize Mary more closely, look desperately into her eyes, and in the perfume of her lips and hair seek anodyne. Between them there was a sufficient store of money, small though it was, to allow them a few months of liberty, undisturbed by any thought of the future. They wandered lazily about Greece for a little time, finding in the Greek day and the immemorial hills a perfect setting for their love.

And yet ever more insistently came to him the call of the hand—the hand which had been his own and not his own, the hand which had united in so unique an embrace his brother with himself.

Again at night voices tormented him. Again, when winds were about, they called with living words, "The hand! The hand! It is calling you, calling! Answer! He wants you! Peter!" wailed the wind. "Peter! Peter!"

Lines began to draw across his forehead. With anxiety Mary saw shadows growing under his eyes, and in his eyes a hunger which grew more and more forlorn. "What is it, love?" she would murmur. "You've not slept well!"

"Nothing at all, love, nothing! All's well!" he would reply, trying with a kiss to forget the wind and the hand and the call.

"There's something you're longing for. Tell me, Ivan. Let me help you. You must."

"Nothing, Mary. I've got you. There's nothing else in the world." But the call of the hand did not abate. "Peter!" the winds wailed, "Peter! He wants you! Answer!"

The urgency of the call grew more imperious. He was sickening and growing weak. There was a hot torpidity in the dry Greek noon which shriveled his veins. He would drag his coat down from his neck and lift his head and try to breathe the deep breath he had known in his Serbian wood. But there was no spaciousness, no great drafts of cool air in the wind, only voices, "Peter! Peter! Peter!"

"We must go somewhere. We must go away," said

The Call of the Hand

Mary. "We must go to Athens and see a doctor, Ivan. I'm afraid!"

"Not Athens! No!" he replied with a shudder, his temples contracting as before the hot blast from an oven. Those dry marble spaces! The dusty pepper trees! The sweating crowds in the shops, swallowing sweet cakes like swine swallowing husks in a sty! Athens became a nightmare.

He was lying awake one night, the body of Mary curled beside him, her hair floating vaguely on the pillow in the half-light of the moon. She stirred in her sleep, and her little white hand unconsciously sought his wrist and fastened tightly round it. That moment bridged the buried time. Unescapably Mary had brought back to him the sensation of Peter lying in the grasp of his own hand. Never before was the call of the hand so imperious. Never so clearly did the wind exclaim, "Peter! He wants you! Answer!"

An irresistible love for his murdered brother overwhelmed him. He raised himself from his bed and lifted helplessly his lopped arm into the whispering room. "Coming, my brother, I am coming! Wait! Peter!" he moaned, and the wind replied, "Peter! Peter!"

He lay back in bed. He realized that the strongest claim in the world upon him was the call of the hand. As for Mary—she was nothing different from himself. For her as for him the call of the hand came dictatorially. In each other they were one, but without the hand their unity was uncompleted. The call of the hand must be obeyed. Tomorrow they must leave Greece behind. Tomorrow to Serbia, tomorrow the response to the hand.

Mary was not surprised when Ivan without warning

explained that all their plans were altered. She was used to his unaccountable whims, the sudden mystic impulses of his Slavonic soul.

They packed up the few things which were all the impediment they possessed, and next day saw them well started on their way to Monastir, carefully skirting Athens. Arrived at Monastir, a few days elapsed before they appeared at the remote wood where Ivan was born. The cottage built by Ivan Kupreloff was not yet occupied. The strange character of its former inhabitants combined with the terrible nature of Peter's death had succeeded in keeping it empty! They obtained permission from its owner to occupy the cottage, and with a great sigh of content Ivan flung open the door where he and his brother had passed so frequently in former days.

In a little time Mary had made of the house such a palace of delight as it had not been since Ivan's mother was dead. Happily, Ivan took in large drafts of the Serbian pineland air, filling his lungs. Happily, with Mary beside him on the bed where he and Peter had lain entwined, the dark drowsy nights melted into dawn. He made his reply to the call of the hand. Only faintly, if at all, the wind or the branches whispered "Peter! Peter!" Peter seemed to be happy at last. The severed hand seemed at last to be tranquil round the wrist of the murdered brother. Then the winds died away, and there was no sound of "Peter!"; only fitfully a swaying of twigs and a rustle of pine needles.

So it seemed. Till summer drooped her drowsing hair. Summer became wrinkled and old. Summer went and the swift autumn came. The days shortened into the rigors of winter, the days ever contracted towards the anniversary of that red day when the axe was lifted and Peter fell. Never for a moment did it occur to Ivan that now when the fatal day was approaching he might leave behind him his Serbian wood. He knew that, more tightly than ever during his living days, the wrist of Peter lay within his own hand, tight, unescapable. Mary and he lay under the thumb of that severed hand wherefrom the red arrow glowed when the night was dark and the woodfire threw leaping shadows over the log walls. There was no gainsaying the call of the hand till the end of days. Ivan knew that never again would he leave behind his Serbian wood.

Came the night which was the anniversary of that dead, unburyable night when Peter's doom had been sealed. Again there was the rumbling of thunder, there were evil flashes of lightning that ran among the clouds. Never with so firm an embrace had Mary been clasped within his arms. Nothing in the world was so strong as his love for Mary. They had responded to the call of the hand. There was no further claim upon them. Ivan kissed her sleeping eyes and was lulled in the music of her breathing. A drowsiness came over him, and for a time he slid into sleep.

In his sleep something tightened round him, something growing so tight that it forced through the barriers of his sleep. Vaguely, faintly a half-consciousness came back to him. He was not awake. He was not asleep. He was in a borderland where the other world is not dead and this world is half-alive. Tighter grew the thing which pressed against his sleep. It was round his wrist, it was round the wrist where something had once come crashing down. What was it? What was it had come crashing down? An axe it was that had come crashing down. It was the hand of Mary growing tighter round his wrist. No, it could not be the hand of Mary. Mary had fallen from his arms. Mary was turned away from him. He could see her hands pale where she had lifted them in sleep above her head. It was not the hand of Mary growing tighter round his wrist. But it was a hand. No doubt of that. It was a hand. With a dull glow of flame a little red arrow gleamed like embers below the thumb of the hand. Where had he seen that arrow? Where and when? When his hand had fallen away from him, lopped at the wrist. It was the dead hand which was not dead. It was his own hand. It was the hand with the red arrow which had held Peter so tightly. It was the dead hand which was alive, the living hand which had arisen from the dead. Tighter round his wrist grew the pressure of the severed hand. The hand was tired of calling. The hand had come. There was no gainsaying the hand. So tight grew the clutch of the hand that his whole arm slowly lifted from his side. Irresistibly the shoulder followed the rising arm. There was no gainsaying the hand. Neither awake nor asleep, neither living nor dead, he followed the hand, he rose from the bed where Mary lay, sleeping sundered from him, his no more. Mary was alive. He was neither living nor dead. The door of the room was opened wide. Closed doors were no barrier against the hand which had arisen from the grave. Slowly, with steady feet, with wide, filmy eyes, Ivan passed through the door. Slowly through the outer door, slowly into the sound of thunder, into the gleam of lightning and the voices of winds moaning unceasingly, "Peter! Peter! He is calling you! Ivan! Peter is calling you! Follow!" and ever again unceasingly, "Peter! Peter!"

The Call of the Hand

Tighter than the bonds of ice or granite hills, tight only as the bond of death, the arisen hand held the lopped wrist, drew the slow body of Ivan through the haunted night far into the wood, far through the talking trees, far to the place of that tree which had not been cut down, to the place where an axe had fallen through bones and flesh, where Peter had fallen, where Peter lay buried, not deep down; where Peter lay buried under twigs and loose earth.

Tightly round the wrist of the man neither alive nor dead clutched the resurrected hand. Nearer and nearer to the shallow grave the hand pulled down the body of Ivan. Methodically, steadily, working with no pause, the free hand of Ivan moved the twigs and the loose earth—methodically, with no pause, until at last the body of Peter lay revealed; not recognizable, dissolute beneath the change through which all men shall pass, recognizable only to those filmy eyes of Ivan, to that questing hungry soul of Ivan which had come to claim its own. Closer and closer to the dead brother the severed hand drew the body of Ivan down; so close, so close, until at last the hand clutched again and for ever that wrist to which Fate had fastened it long years ago. Alongside of his dead brother, quietly, with those eyes which neither saw nor did not see, Ivan lay down full length. Gradually the severed hand, the hand which had arisen from the dead to claim him, because the dead brother called and the severed hand called for its own, gradually the hand slipped from the lopped wrist; the wrist and the arm became one. The hand of Ivan had brought Ivan to his own. Indissolubly, Peter and Ivan lay joined together. But the death which lay cold in the heart and body of Peter passed from the clutched wrist, passed into the hand which clutched it, passed along the arm which had been severed once, and along Ivan's shoulder, until it made of his eyes unseeing discs and his heart cold stone which could beat no more.

As the gray light of dawn came emptily down the Serbian woods, the two brothers lay immortally one again, like the two babies the gods had given Nikolai Kupreloff upon a long-vanished night.

The Dream Woman

by W. Wilkie Collins

When the candle flamed up, the woman with the knife had gone.

I

I had not been settled much more than six weeks in my country practice, when I was sent for to a neighboring town to consult with the resident medical man there, on a case of very dangerous illness.

My horse had come down with me, at the end of a long ride the night before, and had hurt himself, luckily, much more than he had hurt his master. Being deprived of the animal's services, I started for my destination by the coach (there were no railways at that time); and I hoped to get back again, towards the afternoon, in the same way.

After the consultation was over I went to the principal inn of the town to wait for the coach. When it came up, it was full inside and out. There was no resource left me, but to get home as cheaply as I could, by hiring a gig. The price asked for this accommodation struck me as being so extortionate, that I determined to look out for an inn of inferior pretensions, and to try if I could not make a better bargain with a less prosperous establishment.

I soon found a likely-looking house, dingy and quiet, with an old-fashioned sign, that had evidently not been repainted for many years past. The landlord, in this case, was not above making a small profit; and as soon as we came to terms, he rang the yard-bell to order the gig.

"Has Robert not come back from that errand?" asked the landlord appealing to the waiter, who answered the bell.

"No, sir, he hasn't."

"Well, then, you must wake up Isaac."

"Wake up Isaac?" I repeated, "that sounds rather odd. Do your ostlers go to bed in the daytime?"

"This one does," said the landlord, smiling to himself in rather a strange way.

"And dreams, too," added the waiter.

"Never you mind about that," retorted his master, "you go and rouse Isaac up. The gentleman's waiting for his gig."

The landlord's manner and the waiter's manner expressed a great deal more than they either of them said. I began to suspect that I might be on the trace of something professionally interesting to me, as a medical man; and I thought I should like to look at the ostler, before the waiter awakened him.

"Stop a minute," I interposed, "I have rather a fancy for seeing this man before you wake him up. I am a doctor; and if this queer sleeping and dreaming of his comes from anything wrong in his brain, I may be able to tell you what to do with him."

"I rather think you will find his complaint past all doctoring, sir," said the landlord. "But if you would like to see him, you're welcome, I'm sure."

He led the way across a yard and down a passage to the stables; opened one of the doors; and waiting outside himself, told me to look in.

I found myself in a two-stall stable. In one of the stalls, a horse was munching his corn. In the other, an old man was lying asleep on the litter.

I stooped, and looked at him attentively. It was a withered, woebegone face. The eyebrows were painfully contracted; the mouth was fast set, and drawn down at the corners. The hollow wrinkled cheeks, and the scanty grizzled hair, told their own tale of past sorrow or suffering. He was drawing his breath convulsively when I first looked at him; and in a moment more he began to talk in his sleep.

"Wake up!" I heard him say, in a quick whisper, through his clenched teeth. "Wake up, there! Murder."

He moved one lean arm slowly till it rested over his throat, shuddered a little, and turned on the straw. Then the arm left his throat, the hand stretched itself out, and clutched at the side towards which he had turned, as if he fancied himself to be grasping at the edge of something. I saw his lips move, and bent lower over him. He was still talking in his sleep.

"Light gray eyes," he murmured, "and a droop in the left eyelid—flaxen hair, with a gold-yellow streak in it—all right, mother—fair white arms, with a down on them—little lady's hand, with a reddish look under the fingernails. The knife—always the cursed knife—first on one side, then on the other. Aha! you she-devil, where's the knife?"

At the last word his voice rose, and he grew restless of a sudden. I saw him shudder on the straw; his withered face became distorted, and he threw up both his hands with a quick hysterical gasp. They struck against the bottom of the manger under which he lay, and the blow awakened him. I had just time to slip through the door, and close it, before his eyes were fairly open, and his senses his own again.

"Do you know anything about that man's past life?" I said to the landlord.

"Yes, sir, I know pretty well all about it," was the answer, "and an uncommon queer story it is. Most people don't believe it. It's true, though, for all that. Why, just look at him," continued the landlord, opening the stable door again. "Poor devil! he's so worn out with his restless nights, that he's dropped back into his sleep already."

"Don't wake him," I said, "I'm in no hurry for the gig. Wait till the other man comes back from his errand. And in the meantime, suppose I have some lunch, and a bottle of sherry; and suppose you come and help me to get through it."

The heart of mine host, as I had anticipated, warmed to me over his own wine. He soon became communicative on the subject of the man asleep in the stable; and by little and little, I drew the whole story out of him. Extravagant and incredible as the events must appear to everybody, they are related here just as I heard them, and just as they happened.

2

Some years ago there lived in the suburbs of a large seaport town, on the west coast of England, a man in humble circumstances, by the name of Isaac Scatchard. His means of subsistence were derived from any employment he could get as an ostler, and occasionally, when times went well with him, from temporary engagements in service as stable-helper in private houses. Though a faithful, steady, and honest man, he got on badly in his calling. His ill-luck was proverbial among his neighbors. He was always missing good opportunities by no fault of his own; and always living longest in service with amiable people who were not punctual payers of wages. "Unlucky Isaac" was his nickname in his own neighborhood—and no one could say that he did not richly deserve it.

With far more than one man's fair share of adversity to endure, Isaac had but one consolation to support him —and that was of the dreariest and most negative kind. He had no wife and children to increase his anxieties and add to the bitterness of his various failures in life. It might have been from mere insensibility, or it might have been from generous unwillingness to involve another in his own unlucky destiny—but the fact undoubtedly was, that he had arrived at the middle term of life without marrying; and, what is much more remarkable, without once exposing himself, from eighteen to eight-and-thirty, to the genial imputation of ever having had a sweetheart.

When he was out of service, he lived alone with his widowed mother. Mrs. Scatchard was a woman above the average in her lowly station, as to capacity and manners. She had seen better days, as the phrase is; but she never referred to them in the presence of curious visitors; and, though perfectly polite to everyone who approached her, never cultivated any intimacies among her neighbors. She contrived to provide, hardly enough, for her simple wants, by doing rough work for the tailors; and always managed to keep a decent home for her son to return to, whenever his ill-luck drove him out helpless into the world.

One bleak autumn, when Isaac was getting on fast towards forty, and when he was, as usual, out of place through no fault of his own, he set forth from his mother's cottage on a long walk inland to a gentleman's seat, where he had heard that a stable-helper was required.

It wanted then but two days of his birthday; and Mrs. Scatchard, with her usual fondness, made him promise, before he started, that he would be back in time to keep that anniversary with her, in as festive a way as their poor means would allow. It was easy for him to comply with this request, even supposing he slept a night each way on the road.

He was to start from home on Monday morning; and whether he got the new place or not, he was to be back for his birthday dinner on Wednesday at two o'clock.

Arriving at his destination too late on the Monday night to make application for the stable-helper's place, he slept at the village inn, and, in good time on the Tuesday morning, presented himself at the gentleman's house, to fill the vacant situation. Here again, his ill-luck pursued him as inexorably as ever. The excellent written testimonials to his character which he was able to produce, availed him nothing; his long walk had been taken in vain—only the day before, the stable-helper's place had been given to another man.

Isaac accepted this new disappointment resignedly, and as a matter of course. Naturally slow in capacity, he had the bluntness of sensibility and phlegmatic patience of disposition which frequently distinguish men with sluggishly-working mental powers. He thanked the gentleman's steward with his usual quiet civility, for granting him an interview, and took his departure with no appearance of unusual depression in his face or manner.

Before starting on his homeward walk, he made some inquiries at the inn, and ascertained that he might save a few miles, on his return, by following a new road. Furnished with full instructions, several times repeated, as to the various turnings he was to take, he set forth on his homeward journey, and walked on all day with only one stoppage for bread and cheese. Just as it was getting towards dark, the rain came on and the wind began to rise; and he found himself, to make matters worse, in a part of the country with which he was entirely unacquainted, though he knew himself to be some fifteen miles from home. The first house he found to inquire at, was a lonely roadside inn, standing on the outskirts of a thick wood. Solitary as the place looked, it was welcome to a lost man who was also hungry, thirsty, footsore, and wet. The landlord was civil and respectable-looking, and the price he asked for a bed was reasonable enough. Isaac therefore decided on stopping comfortably at the inn for that night.

He was constitutionally a temperate man. His supper simply consisted of two rashers of bacon, a slice of home-made bread, and a pint of ale. He did not go to bed immediately after this moderate meal, but sat up with the landlord, talking about his bad prospects and his long run of ill-luck, and diverging from these topics to the subjects of horseflesh and racing. Nothing was said either by himself, his host, or the few laborers who strayed into the taproom, which could, in the slightest degree, excite the very small and very dull imaginative faculty which Isaac Scatchard possessed.

At a little after eleven the house was closed. Isaac went round with the landlord, and held the candle while the doors and lower windows were being secured. He noticed with surprise the strength of the bolts, bars, and iron-sheathed shutters.

"You see, we are rather lonely here," said the landlord. "We never have had any attempts made to break in yet, but it's always as well to be on the safe side. When nobody is sleeping here I am the only man in the house. My wife and daughter are timid, and the servant-girl takes after her missuses. Another glass of ale, before you turn in?—No!—Well, how such a sober man as you comes to be out of place, is more than I can make out, for one—Here's where you're to sleep. You're the only lodger tonight, and I think you'll say my missus has done her best to make you comfortable. You won't have another glass of ale?—Very well. Good night."

It was half past eleven by the clock in the passage as they went upstairs to the bedroom, the window of which looked on to the wood at the back of the house.

Isaac locked the door, set his candle on the chest of drawers, and wearily got ready for bed. The bleak autumn wind was still blowing, and the solemn surging moan of it in the wood was dreary and awful to hear through the night-silence. Isaac felt strangely wakeful. He resolved, as he lay down in bed, to keep the candle alight until he began to grow sleepy; for there was something unendurably depressing in the bare idea of lying awake in the darkness, listening to the dismal, ceaseless moan of the wind in the wood.

Sleep stole on him before he was aware of it. His eyes closed, and he fell off insensibly to rest, without having so much as thought of extinguishing the candle.

The first sensation of which he was conscious, after sinking into slumber, was a strange shivering that ran through him suddenly from head to foot, and a dreadful sinking pain at the heart, such as he had never felt before. The shivering only disturbed his slumbers—the pain woke him instantly. In one moment he passed from a state of sleep to a state of wakefulness—his eyes wide open—his mental perceptions cleared on a sudden as if by a miracle.

The candle had burnt down nearly to the last morsel of tallow, but the top of the unsnuffed wick had just fallen off, and the light in the little room was, for the moment, fair and full.

Between the foot of the bed and the closed door, there stood a woman with a knife in her hand, looking at him.

He was stricken speechless with terror, but he did not lose the preternatural clearness of his faculties; and he never took his eyes off the woman. She said not a word as they stared each other in the face; but she began to move slowly towards the left-hand side of the bed.

His eyes followed her. She was a fair fine woman, with yellowish flaxen hair, and light gray eyes, with a droop in the left eyelid. He noticed these things and fixed them on his mind, before she was round at the side of the bed. Speechless, with no expression in her face, with no noise following her footfall, she came closer and closer—stopped—and slowly raised the knife. He laid his right arm over his throat to save it; but, as he saw the knife coming down, threw his hand across the bed to the right side, and jerked his body over that way, just as the knife descended on the mattress within an inch of his shoulder.

His eyes fixed on her arm and hand, as she slowly drew her knife out of the bed. A white, well-shaped arm, with a pretty down lying lightly over the fair skin. A delicate, lady's hand, with the crowning beauty of a pink flush under and round the fingernails.

She drew the knife out, and passed back again slowly to the foot of the bed; stopped there for a moment looking at him; then came on—still speechless, still with no expression on the beautiful face, still with no sound following the stealthy footfalls—came on to the right side of the bed where he now lay.

As she approached, she raised the knife again, and he drew himself away to the left side. She struck, as before, right into the mattress, with a deliberate, perpendicularly downward action of the arm. This time his eyes wandered from her to the knife. It was like the large clasp-knives which he had often seen laboring men use to cut their bread and bacon with. Her delicate little fingers did not conceal more than two-thirds of the handle; he noticed that it was made of buckhorn, clean and shining as the blade was, and looking like new.

For the second time she drew the knife out, concealed it in the wide sleeve of her gown, then stopped by the bedside, watching him. For an instant he saw her standing in that position—then the wick of the spent candle fell over into the socket. The flame diminished to a little blue point, and the room grew dark.

The Dream Woman

A moment, or less if possible, passed so—and then the wick flamed up, smokily, for the last time. His eyes were still looking eagerly over the right-hand side of the bed when the final flash of light came, but they discerned nothing. The fair woman with the knife was gone.

The conviction that he was alone again, weakened the hold of the terror that had struck him dumb up to this time. The preternatural sharpness which the very intensity of his panic had mysteriously imparted to his faculties, left them suddenly. His brain grew confused —his heart beat wildly—his ears opened for the first time since the appearance of the woman, to a sense of the woeful, ceaseless moaning of the wind among the trees. With the dreadful conviction of the reality of what he had seen still strong within him, he leapt out of bed, and screaming—"Murder!—Wake up there, wake up!"—dashed headlong through the darkness to the door.

It was fast locked, exactly as he had left it on going to bed.

His cries, on starting up, had alarmed the house. He heard the terrified, confused exclamations of women; he saw the master of the house approaching along the passage, with his burning rush-candle in one hand and his gun in the other.

"What is it?" asked the landlord, breathlessly.

Isaac could only answer in a whisper. "A woman, with a knife in her hand," he gasped out. "In my room— a fair, yellow-haired woman; she jabbed at me with the knife, twice over."

The landlord's pale cheek grew paler. He looked at Isaac eagerly by the flickering light of his candle; and his face began to get red again—his voice altered, too, as well as his complexion.

"She seems to have missed you twice," he said.

"I dodged the knife as it came down," Isaac went on, in the same scared whisper. "It struck the bed each time."

The landlord took his candle into the bedroom immediately. In less than a minute he came out again into the passage in a violent passion.

"The devil fly away with you and your woman with the knife! There isn't a mark in the bedclothes anywhere. What do you mean by coming into a man's place and frightening his family out of their wits by a dream?"

"I'll leave your house," said Isaac, faintly. "Better out on the road, in rain and dark, on my way home, than back again in that room, after what I've seen in it. Lend me a light to get my clothes by, and tell me what I'm to pay."

"Pay!" cried the landlord, leading the way with his light sulkily into the bedroom. "You'll find your score on the slate when you go downstairs. I wouldn't have taken you in for all the money you've got about you, if I'd known your dreaming, screeching ways beforehand. Look at the bed. Where's the cut of a knife in it? Look at the window—is the lock bursted? Look at the door (which I heard you fasten yourself)—is it broke in? A murdering woman with a knife in my house! You ought to be ashamed of yourself!"

Isaac answered not a word. He huddled on his clothes; and then they went down the stairs together.

"Nigh on twenty minutes past two!" said the landlord, as they passed the clock. "A nice time in the morning to frighten honest people out of their wits!"

Isaac paid his bill, and the landlord let him out at the front door, asking, with a grin of contempt, as he undid the strong fastenings, whether "the murdering woman got in that way?"

They parted without a word on either side. The rain had ceased; but the night was dark, and the wind bleaker than ever. Little did the darkness, or the cold, or the uncertainty about the way home matter to Isaac. If he had been turned out into the wilderness in a thunderstorm, it would have been a relief, after what he had suffered in the bedroom of the inn.

What was the fair woman with the knife? The creature of a dream, or that other creature from the unknown world, called among men by the name of ghost? He could make nothing of the mystery—had made nothing of it, even when it was midday on Wednesday, and when he stood, at last, after many times missing his road, once more on the doorstep of home.

3

His mother came out eagerly to receive him. His face told her in a moment that something was wrong.

"I've lost the place, but that's my luck. I dreamed an ill dream last night, mother—or, maybe, I saw a ghost. Take it either way, it scared me out of my senses, and I'm not my own man again yet."

"Isaac! Your face frightens me. Come in to the fire. Come in, and tell mother all about it."

He was as anxious to tell as she was to hear; for it had been his hope, all the way home, that his mother, with her quicker capacity and superior knowledge, might be able to throw some light on the mystery which he could not clear up for himself. His memory of the dream was still mechanically vivid, though his thoughts were entirely confused by it.

His mother's face grew paler and paler as he went on. She never interrupted him by so much as a single word; but when he had done, she moved her chair close to his, put her arm around his neck, and said to him,

"Isaac, you dreamed your ill dream on this Wednesday morning. What time was it when you saw the fair woman with the knife in her hand?"

Isaac reflected on what the landlord had said when they had passed by the clock on his leaving the inn—allowed as nearly as he could for the time that must have elapsed between the unlocking of his bedroom door and the paying of his bill just before going away, and answered,

"Somewhere about two o'clock in the morning."

His mother suddenly quitted her hold of his neck, and struck her hands together with a gesture of despair.

"This Wednesday is your birthday, Isaac; and two o'clock in the morning is the time when you were born!"

Isaac's capacities were not quick enough to catch the infection of his mother's superstitious dread. He was amazed, and a little startled also, when she suddenly rose from her chair, opened her old writing desk, took pen, ink, and paper, and then said to him—

"Your memory is but a poor one, Isaac, and now I'm an old woman, mine's not much better. I want all about this dream of yours to be as well known to both of us, years hence, as it is now. Tell me over again all you told

The Dream Woman

me a minute ago, when you spoke of what the woman with the knife looked like."

Isaac obeyed, and marveled much as he saw his mother carefully set down on paper the very words that he was saying.

"Light gray eyes," she wrote as they came to the descriptive part, "with a droop in the left eyelid. Flaxen hair, with a gold-yellow streak in it. White arms, with a down upon them. Little lady's hand, with a reddish look about the fingernails. Clasp-knife with a buckhorn handle, that seemed as good as new." To these particulars, Mrs. Scatchard added the year, month, day of the week, and time in the morning, when the woman of the dream appeared to her son. She then locked up the paper carefully in her writing desk.

Neither on that day, nor on any day after, could her son induce her to return to the matter of the dream. She obstinately kept her thoughts about it to herself, and even refused to refer again to the paper in her writing desk. Ere long, Isaac grew weary of attempting to make her break her resolute silence; and time, which sooner or later wears out all things, gradually wore out the impression produced on him by the dream. He began by thinking of it carelessly, and he ended by not thinking of it at all.

This result was the more easily brought about by the advent of some important changes for the better in his prospects, which commenced not long after his terrible night's experience at the inn. He reaped at last the reward of his long and patient suffering under adversity, by getting an excellent place, keeping it for seven years, and leaving it, on the death of his master, not only with an excellent character, but also with a comfortable annuity bequeathed to him as a reward for saving his mistress's life in a carriage accident. Thus it happened that Isaac Scatchard returned to his old mother, seven years after the time of the dream at the inn, with an annual sum of money at his disposal, sufficient to keep them both in ease and independence for the rest of their lives.

The mother, whose health had been bad of late years, profited so much by the care bestowed on her and by freedom from money anxieties, that when Isaac's birthday came round, she was able to sit up comfortably at table and dine with him.

On that day, as the evening drew on, Mrs. Scatchard discovered that a bottle of tonic medicine—which she was accustomed to take, and in which she had fancied that a dose or more was still left—happened to be empty. Isaac immediately volunteered to go to the chemist's and get it filled again. It was as rainy and bleak an autumn night as on the memorable past occasion when he lost his way and slept at the roadside inn.

On going into the chemist's shop, he was passed hurriedly by a poorly-dressed woman coming out of it. The glimpse he had of her face struck him, and he looked back after her as she descended the doorsteps.

"You're noticing that woman?" said the chemist's apprentice behind the counter. "It's my opinion there's something wrong with her. She's been asking for laudanum to put to a bad tooth. Master's out for half an hour; and I told her I wasn't allowed to sell poison to strangers in his absence. She laughed in a queer way, and said she would come back in half an hour. If she expects

The Dream Woman 85

master to serve her, I think she'll be disappointed. It's a case of suicide, sir, if ever there was one yet."

These words added immeasurably to the sudden interest in the woman which Isaac had felt at the first sight of her face. After he had got the medicine bottle filled, he looked about anxiously for her, as soon as he was out in the street. She was walking slowly up and down on the opposite side of the road. With his heart, very much to his own surprise, beating fast, Isaac crossed over and spoke to her.

He asked if she was in any distress. She pointed to her torn shawl, her scanty dress, her crushed, dirty bonnet—then moved under a lamp so as to let the light fall on her stern, pale, but still most beautiful face.

"I look like a comfortable, happy woman—don't I?" she said, with a bitter laugh.

She spoke with a purity of intonation which Isaac had never heard before from other than ladies' lips. Her slightest actions seemed to have the easy, negligent grace of a thoroughbred woman. Her skin, for all its poverty-stricken paleness, was as delicate as if her life had been passed in the enjoyment of every social comfort that wealth can purchase. Even her small, finely shaped hands, gloveless as they were, had not lost their whiteness.

Little by little, in answer to his questions, the sad story of the woman came out. There is no need to relate it here; it is told over and over again in police reports and paragraphs descriptive of attempted suicides.

"My name is Rebecca Murdoch," said the woman, as she ended. "I have ninepence left, and I thought of spending it at the chemist's over the way in securing a passage to the other world. Whatever it is, it can't be worse to me than this—so why should I stop here?"

Besides the natural compassion and sadness moved in his heart by what he heard, Isaac felt within him some mysterious influence at work all the time the woman was speaking, which utterly confused his ideas and almost deprived him of his powers of speech. All that he could say in answer to her last reckless words was, that he would prevent her from attempting her own life, if he followed her about all night to do it. His rough, trembling earnestness seemed to impress her.

"I won't occasion you that trouble," she answered, when he repeated his threat. "You have given me a fancy for living by speaking kindly to me. No need for the mockery of protestations and promises. You may believe me without them. Come to Fuller's Meadow tomorrow at twelve, and you will find me alive, to answer for myself. No!—no money. My ninepence will do to get me as good a night's lodging as I want."

She nodded and left him. He made no attempt to follow—he felt no suspicion that she was deceiving him.

"It's strange, but I can't help believing her," he said to himself, and walked away bewildered towards home.

On entering the house, his mind was still so completely absorbed by its new subject of interest, that he took no notice of what his mother was doing when he came in with the bottle of medicine. She had opened her old writing desk in his absence, and was now reading a paper attentively that lay inside it. On every birthday of Isaac's since she had written down the particulars of his dream from his own lips, she had been accustomed to read that same paper, and ponder over it in private.

The next day he went to Fuller's Meadow.

The Dream Woman

He had done only right in believing her so implicitly—she was there, punctual to a minute, to answer for herself. The last-left faint defenses in Isaac's heart, against the fascination which a word or look from her began inscrutably to exercise over him, sank down and vanished before her forever on that memorable morning.

When a man, previously insensible to the influence of women, forms an attachment in middle life, the instances are rare indeed, let the warning circumstances be what they may, in which he is found capable of freeing himself from the tyranny of the new ruling passion. The charm of being spoken to familiarly, fondly, and gratefully by a woman whose language and manners still retained enough of their early refinement to hint at the high social station that she had lost, would have been a dangerous luxury to a man of Isaac's rank at the age of twenty. But it was far more than that—it was certain ruin to him—now that his heart was opening unworthily to a new influence at the middle time of life when strong feelings of all kinds, once implanted, strike root most stubbornly in a man's moral nature. A few more stolen interviews after that first morning in Fuller's Meadow completed his infatuation. In less than a month from the time when he first met her, Isaac Scatchard had consented to give Rebecca Murdoch a new interest in existence, and a chance of recovering the character she had lost, by promising to make her his wife.

She had taken possession not of his passions only, but of his faculties as well. All the mind he had he put into her keeping. She directed him on every point, even instructing him how to break the news of his approaching marriage in the safest manner to his mother.

"If you tell her how you met me and who I am at first," said the cunning woman, "she will move heaven and earth to prevent our marriage. Say I am the sister of one of your fellow-servants—ask her to see me before you go into any more particulars—and leave it to me to do the rest. I mean to make her love me next best to you, Isaac, before she knows anything of who I really am."

The motive of the deceit was sufficient to sanctify it to Isaac. The stratagem proposed relieved him of his one great anxiety, and quieted his uneasy conscience on the subject of his mother. Still, there was something wanting to perfect his happiness, something that he could not realize, something mysteriously untraceable, and yet something that perpetually made itself felt—not when he was absent from Rebecca Murdoch, but, strange to say, when he was actually in her presence! She was kindness itself with him; she never made him feel his inferior capacities and inferior manners—she showed the sweetest anxiety to please him in the smallest trifles; but, in spite of all these attractions, he never could feel quite at his ease with her. At their first meeting, there had mingled with his admiration when he looked in her face, a faint involuntary feeling of doubt whether that face was entirely strange to him. No after-familiarity had the slightest effect on this inexplicable, wearisome uncertainty.

Concealing the truth, as he had been directed, he announced his marriage engagement precipitately and confusedly to his mother, on the day when he contracted it. Poor Mrs. Scatchard showed her perfect confidence in her son by flinging her arms round his neck, and giving him joy of having found at last, in the sister of one of his fellow-servants, a woman to comfort and care

The Dream Woman

for him after his mother was gone. She was all eagerness to see the woman of her son's choice; and the next day was fixed for the introduction.

It was a bright sunny morning, and the little cottage parlor was full of light, as Mrs. Scatchard, happy and expectant, dressed for the occasion in her Sunday gown, sat waiting for her son and her future daughter-in-law.

Punctual to the appointed time, Isaac hurriedly and nervously led his promised wife into the room. His mother rose to receive her—advanced a few steps, smiling—looked Rebecca full in the eyes—and suddenly stopped. Her face, which had been flushed the moment before, turned white in an instant—her eyes lost their expression of softness and kindness, and assumed a blank look of terror—her outstretched hands fell to her sides, and she staggered back a few steps with a low cry to her son.

"Isaac!" she whispered, clutching him fast by the arm, when he asked alarmedly if she was taken ill, "Isaac! does that woman's face remind you of nothing?"

Before he could answer, before he could look round to where Rebecca stood, astonished and angered by her reception, at the lower end of the room, his mother pointed impatiently to her writing desk and gave him the key.

"Open it," she said, in a quick, breathless whisper.

"What does this mean? Why am I treated as if I had no business here? Does your mother want to insult me?" asked Rebecca, angrily.

"Open it, and give me the paper in the left-hand drawer. Quick! quick! for heaven's sake!" said Mrs. Scatchard, shrinking further back in terror.

Isaac gave her the paper. She looked it over eagerly

for a moment—then followed Rebecca, who was now turning away haughtily to leave the room, and caught her by the shoulder—abruptly raised the long, loose sleeve of her gown—and glanced at her hand and arm. Something like fear began to steal over the angry expression of Rebecca's face, as she shook herself free from the old woman's grasp. "Mad!" she said to herself, "and Isaac never told me." With those few words she left the room.

Isaac was hastening after her, when his mother turned and stopped his further progress. It wrung his heart to see the misery and terror in her face as she looked at him.

"Light gray eyes," she said, in low, mournful, awestruck tones, pointing towards the open door. "A droop in the left eyelid; flaxen hair with a gold-yellow streak in it; white arms with a down on them; little, lady's hand, with a reddish look under the fingernails. *The Dream Woman!*—Isaac, the Dream Woman!"

That faint cleaving doubt which he had never been able to shake off in Rebecca Murdoch's presence, was fatally set at rest for ever. He *had* seen her face, then, before—seven years before, on his birthday, in the bedroom of the lonely inn.

"Be warned! Oh, my son, be warned! Isaac! Isaac! let her go, and do you stop with me!"

Something darkened the parlor window as those words were said. A sudden chill ran through him, and he glanced sidelong at the shadow. Rebecca Murdoch had come back. She was peering in curiously at them over the low window blind.

"I have promised to marry, Mother," he said, "and marry I must."

The tears came into his eyes as he spoke, and dimmed his sight; but he could just discern the fatal face outside, moving away again from the window.

His mother's head sank lower.

"Are you faint?" he whispered.

"Brokenhearted, Isaac."

He stooped down and kissed her. The shadow, as he did so, returned to the window; and the fatal face peered in curiously once more.

4

Three weeks after that day Isaac and Rebecca were man and wife. All that was hopelessly dogged and stubborn in the man's moral nature, seemed to have closed round his fatal passion, and to have fixed it unassailably in his heart.

After that first interview in the cottage parlor, no consideration could induce Mrs. Scatchard to see her son's wife again, or even to talk of her when Isaac tried hard to plead her cause after their marriage.

This course of conduct was not in any degree occasioned by a discovery of the degradation in which Rebecca had lived. There was no question of that between mother and son. There was no question of anything but the fearfully exact resemblance between the living, breathing woman, and the spectre-woman of Isaac's dream.

Rebecca, on her side, neither felt nor expressed the slightest sorrow at the estrangement between herself and her mother-in-law. Isaac, for the sake of peace, had never contradicted her first idea that age and long illness had affected Mrs. Scatchard's mind. He even allowed his wife to upbraid him for not having confessed this to her at the time of their marriage engagement, rather than risk anything by hitting at the truth. The sacrifice of his integrity before his one all-mastering delusion, seemed but a small thing, and cost his conscience but little, after the sacrifices he had already made.

The time of waking from his delusion—the cruel and the rueful time—was not far off. After some quiet months of married life, as the summer was ending, and the year was getting on towards the month of his birthday, Isaac found his wife altering towards him. She grew sullen and contemptuous; she formed acquaintances of the most dangerous kind, in defiance of his objections, his entreaties, and his commands; and, worst of all, she learned, ere long, after every fresh difference with her husband, to seek the deadly self-oblivion of drink. Little by little, after the first miserable discovery that his wife was keeping company with drunkards, the shocking certainty forced itself on Isaac that she had grown to be a drunkard herself.

He had been in a sadly desponding state for some time before the occurrence of these domestic calamities. His mother's health, as he could but too plainly discern every time he went to see her at the cottage, was failing fast; and he upbraided himself in secret as the cause of the bodily and mental suffering she endured. When to his remorse on his mother's account was added the shame and misery occasioned by the discovery of his wife's degradation, he sank under the double trial, his face began to alter fast, and he looked, what he was, a spirit-broken man.

His mother, still struggling bravely against the illness

that was hurrying her to the grave, was the first to notice the sad alteration in him, and the first to hear of his last, worst trouble with his wife. She could only weep bitterly, on the day when he made his humiliating confession; but on the next occasion when he went to see her, she had taken a resolution, in reference to his domestic afflictions, which astonished, and even alarmed him. He found her dressed to go out, and on asking the reason, received this answer:

"I am not long for this world, Isaac," she said; "and I shall not feel easy on my deathbed, unless I have done my best to the last to make my son happy. I mean to put my own fears and my own feelings out of the question, and to go with you to your wife, and try what I can do to reclaim her. Give me your arm, Isaac, and let me do the last thing I can in this world to help my son, before it is too late."

He could not disobey her; and they walked together slowly towards his miserable home.

It was only one o'clock in the afternoon when they reached the cottage where he lived. It was their dinner hour, and Rebecca was in the kitchen. He was thus able to take his mother quietly into the parlor, and then prepare his wife for the interview. She had fortunately drunk but little at that early hour, and she was less sullen and capricious than usual.

He returned to his mother, with his mind tolerably at ease. His wife soon followed him into the parlor, and the meeting between her and Mrs. Scatchard passed off better than he had ventured to anticipate; though he observed with secret apprehension that his mother, resolutely as she controlled herself in other respects, could not look his wife in the face when she spoke to her. It was a relief to him, therefore, when Rebecca began to lay the cloth.

She laid the cloth, brought in the bread-tray, and cut a slice from the loaf for her husband, then returned to the kitchen. At that moment, Isaac, still anxiously watching his mother, was startled by seeing the same ghastly change pass over her face which had altered it so awfully on the morning when Rebecca and she first met. Before he could say a word, she whispered with a look of horror,

"Take me back!—home, home again, Isaac! Come with me, and never go back again!"

He was afraid to ask for an explanation; he could only sign her to be silent, and help her quickly to the door. As they passed the bread-tray on the table, she stopped and pointed to it.

"Did you see what your wife cut your bread with?" she asked in a low whisper.

"No, Mother; I was not noticing. What was it?"

"Look!"

He did look. A new clasp-knife, with a buckhorn handle, lay with the loaf in the bread-tray. He stretched out his hand, shudderingly, to possess himself of it; but at the same time, there was a noise in the kitchen, and his mother caught at his arm.

"The knife of the dream! Isaac, I'm faint with fear— take me away, before she comes back!"

He was hardly able to support her. The visible, tangible reality of the knife struck him with a panic, and utterly destroyed any faint doubts he might have entertained up to this time, in relation to the mysterious dream-warning of nearly eight years before. By a last desperate effort, he summoned self-possession enough to help his mother out of the house—so quietly, that the "Dream Woman" (he thought of her by that name now) did not hear their departure.

"Don't go back, Isaac, don't go back!" implored Mrs. Scatchard, as he turned to go away, after seeing her safely seated again in her own room.

"I must get the knife," he answered under his breath. His mother tried to stop him again; but he hurried out without another word.

On his return, he found that his wife had discovered their secret departure from the house. She had been drinking, and was in a fury of passion. The dinner in the kitchen was flung under the grate; the cloth was off the parlor table. Where was the knife?

Unwisely, he asked for it. She was only too glad of the opportunity of irritating him, which the request afforded her. "He wanted the knife, did he? Could he give her a reason why?—No? Then he should not have it—not if he went down on his knees to ask for it." Further recriminations elicited the fact that she bought it a bargain, and that she considered it her own especial property. Isaac saw the uselessness of attempting to get the knife by fair means, and determined to search for it, later in the day, in secret. The search was unsuccessful. Night came on, and he left the house to walk about the streets. He was afraid now to sleep in the same room with her.

Three weeks passed. Still sullenly enraged with him, she would not give up the knife; and still that fear of sleeping in the same room with her possessed him. He walked about at night, or dozed in the parlor, or sat watching by his mother's bedside. Before the expiration of the first week in the new month his mother died. It wanted then but ten days of her son's birthday. She had longed to live till that anniversary. Isaac was present at her death; and her last words in this world were addressed to him:

"Don't go back, my son—don't go back!"

He was obliged to go back, if it were only to watch his wife. Exasperated to the last degree by his distrust of her, she had revengefully sought to add a sting to his grief, during the last days of his mother's illness, by declaring that she would assert her right to attend the funeral. In spite of all that he could do or say, she held with wicked pertinacity to her words and, on the day appointed for the burial, forced herself—inflamed and shameless with drink—into her husband's presence, and declared that she would walk in the funeral procession to his mother's grave.

This last worst outrage, accompanied by all that was most insulting in word and look, maddened him for the moment. He struck her.

The instant the blow was dealt, he repented it. She crouched down, silent, in a corner of the room, and eyed him steadily; it was a look that cooled his hot blood, and made him tremble. But there was no time now to think of a means of making atonement. Nothing remained but to risk the worst till the funeral was over. There was but one way of making sure of her. He locked her into her bedroom.

When he came back, some hours after, he found her sitting, very much altered in look and bearing, by the bedside, with a bundle on her lap. She rose, and faced him quietly, and spoke with a strange stillness in her voice, a strange repose in her eyes, a strange composure in her manner.

"No man has ever struck me twice," she said; "and my husband shall have no second opportunity. Set the door open and let me go. From this day forth we see each other no more."

Before he could answer she passed him, and left the room. He saw her walk away up the street.

Would she return?

All that night he watched and waited; but no footstep came near the house. The next night, overcome by fatigue, he lay down in bed in his clothes, with the door locked, the key on the table, and the candle burning. His slumber was not disturbed. The third night, the fourth, the fifth, the sixth passed, and nothing happened. He lay down on the seventh, still in his clothes, still with the door locked, the key on the table, and the candle burning; but easier in his mind.

Easier in his mind, and in perfect health of body, when he fell off to sleep. But his rest was disturbed. He woke twice, without any sensation of uneasiness. But the third time it was that never-to-be-forgotten shivering of the night at the lonely inn, that dreadful sinking pain at the heart, which once more aroused him in an instant.

His eyes opened towards the left-hand side of the bed, and there stood—

The Dream Woman again? No! His wife; the living reality, with the dream-spectre's face—in the dream-spectre's attitude: the fair arm up; the knife clasped in the delicate white hand.

He sprang upon her, almost at the instant of seeing

her, and yet not quickly enough to prevent her from hiding the knife. Without a word from him, without a cry from her, he pinioned her in the chair. With one hand he felt up her sleeve; and there, where the Dream Woman had hidden the knife, his wife had hidden it— the knife with the buckhorn handle, that looked like new.

In the despair of that fearful moment his brain was steady, his heart was calm. He looked at her fixedly, with the knife in his hand, and said these last words,

"You told me we should see each other no more, and you have come back. It is my turn now to go, and to go for ever. I say that we shall see each other no more; and *my* word shall not be broken."

He left her, and set forth into the night. There was a bleak wind abroad, and the smell of recent rain was in the air. The distant church clocks chimed the quarter as he walked rapidly beyond the last houses in the suburb. He asked the first policeman he met, what hour that was, of which the quarter past had just struck.

The man referred sleepily to his watch, and answered, "Two o'clock." Two in the morning. What day of the month was this day that had just begun? He reckoned it up from the date of his mother's funeral. The fatal parallel was complete—it was his birthday!

Had he escaped the mortal peril which his dream foretold? Or had he only received a second warning?

As this ominous doubt forced itself on his mind, he stopped, reflected, and turned back again towards the city. He was still resolute to hold his word, and never to let her see him more; but there was a thought now in his mind of having her watched and followed. The knife was in his possession; the world was before him;

but a new distrust of her—a vague, unspeakable, superstitious dread—had overcome him.

"I must know where she goes, now she thinks I have left her," he said to himself, as he stole back wearily to the precincts of his house.

It was still dark. He had left the candle burning in the bedchamber; but when he looked up to the window of the room now, there was no light in it. He crept cautiously to the house door. On going away, he remembered to have closed it; on trying it now, he found it open.

He waited outside, never losing sight of the house till daylight. Then he ventured indoors—listened, and heard nothing—looked into kitchen, scullery, parlor, and found nothing; went up at last into the bedroom—it was empty. A picklock lay on the floor, betraying how she had gained entrance in the night, and that was the only trace of her.

Whither had she gone? No mortal tongue could tell him. The darkness had covered her flight; and when the day broke, no man could say where the light found her.

Before leaving the house and the town for ever, he gave instructions to a friend and neighbor to sell his furniture for anything that it would fetch, and to apply the proceeds towards employing the police to trace her. The directions were honestly followed, and the money was all spent; but the inquiries led to nothing. The picklock on the bedroom floor remained the last useless trace of the Dream Woman.

At this part of the narrative the landlord paused; and, turning towards the window of the room in which we were sitting, looked in the direction of the stable yard.

"So far," he said, "I tell you what was told to me. The little that remains to be added, lies within my own experience. Between two and three months after the events I have just been relating, Isaac Scatchard came to me, withered and old-looking before his time, just as you saw him today. He had his testimonials to character with him, and he asked me for employment here. Knowing that my wife and he were distantly related, I gave him a trial, in consideration of that relationship, and liked him in spite of his queer habits. He is as sober, honest, and willing a man as there is in England. As for his restlessness at night, and his sleeping away his leisure time in the day, who can wonder at it after hearing his story? Besides, he never objects to being roused up, when he's wanted, so there's not much inconvenience to complain of, after all."

"I suppose he is afraid of a return of that dreadful dream, and of waking out of it in the dark?"

"No," returned the landlord. "The dream comes back to him so often, that he has got to bear with it by this time resignedly enough. It's his wife keeps him waking at night, as he often told me."

"What! Has she never been heard of yet?"

"Never. Isaac himself has the one perpetual thought, that she is alive and looking for him. I believe he wouldn't let himself drop off to sleep towards two in the morning for a king's ransom. Two in the morning, he says, is the time she will find him, one of these days. Two in the morning is the time, all the year round, when he likes to be most certain that he has got the clasp-knife safe about him. He does not mind being alone, as long as he is awake, except on the night before his birthday, when he firmly believes himself to be in peril of his life. The birthday has only come round once since he has been here, and then he sat up along with the night-porter. 'She's looking for me,' is all he says, when anybody speaks to him about the one anxiety of his life; 'she's looking for me.' He may be right. She *may* be looking for him. Who can tell?"

"Who can tell?" said I.

The Story of the Late Mr. Elvesham

by H. G. Wells

"I spoke aloud. 'How the devil did I get here?' . . . And the voice was not my own."

I set this story down, not expecting it will be believed, but, if possible, to prepare a way of escape for the next victim. He, perhaps, may profit by my misfortune. My own case, I know, is hopeless, and I am now in some measure prepared to meet my fate.

My name is Edward George Eden. I was born at Trentham, in Staffordshire, my father being employed in the gardens there. I lost my mother when I was three years old, and my father when I was five, my uncle, George Eden, then adopting me as his own son. He was a single man, self-educated, and well-known in Birmingham as an enterprising journalist; he educated me generously, fired my ambition to succeed in the world, and at his death, which happened four years ago, left me his entire fortune, a matter of about five hundred pounds after all outgoing charges were paid. I was then eighteen. He advised me in his will to expend the money in completing my education. I had already chosen the profession of medicine, and through his posthumous generosity and my good fortune in a scholarship competition, I became a medical student at University College, London. At the time of the beginning of my story I lodged at 11A University Street in a little upper room, very shabbily furnished and drafty, overlooking the back of Shoolbred's premises. I used this little room both to live in and sleep in, because I was anxious to eke out my means to the very last shillingsworth.

I was taking a pair of shoes to be mended at a shop in the Tottenham Court Road when I first encountered the little old man with the yellow face, with whom my life has now become so inextricably entangled. He was standing on the curb, and staring at the number on the door in a doubtful way, as I opened it. His eyes—they were dull gray eyes, and reddish under the rims—fell to my face, and his countenance immediately assumed an expression of corrugated amiability.

"You come," he said, "apt to the moment. I had forgotten the number of your house. How do you do, Mr. Eden?"

I was a little astonished at his familiar address, for I had never set eyes on the man before. I was a little annoyed, too, at his catching me with my boots under my arm. He noticed my lack of cordiality.

"Wonder who the deuce I am, eh? A friend, let me assure you. I have seen you before, though you haven't seen me. Is there anywhere where I can talk to you?"

I hesitated. The shabbiness of my room upstairs was not a matter for every stranger. "Perhaps," said I, "we might walk down the street. I'm unfortunately prevented—" My gesture explained the sentence before I had spoken it.

"The very thing," he said, and faced this way, and then that. "The street? Which way shall we go?" I slipped my boots down in the passage. "Look here!" he said abruptly; "this business of mine is a rigmarole. Come and lunch with me, Mr. Eden. I'm an old man, a very old man, and not good at explanations, and what with my piping voice and the clatter of the traffic—"

He laid a persuasive skinny hand that trembled a little upon my arm.

I was not so old that an old man might not treat me to a lunch. Yet at the same time I was not altogether pleased by this abrupt invitation. "I had rather—" I began. "But I had rather," he said, catching me up, "and a certain civility is surely due to my gray hairs."

And so I consented, and went with him.

He took me to Blavitiski's; I had to walk slowly to accommodate myself to his paces; and over such a lunch as I had never tasted before, he fended off my leading questions, and I took a better note of his appearance. His clean-shaven face was lean and wrinkled, his shriveled lips fell over a set of false teeth, and his white hair was thin and rather long; he seemed small to me— though, indeed, most people seemed small to me—and his shoulders were rounded and bent. And watching him, I could not help but observe that he too was taking note of me, running his eyes, with a curious touch of greed in them, over me, from my broad shoulders to my suntanned hands, and up to my freckled face again. "And now," said he, as we lit our cigarettes, "I must tell you of the business in hand.

"I must tell you, then, that I am an old man, a very

The Story of the Late Mr. Elvesham

old man." He paused momentarily. "And it happens that I have money that I must presently be leaving, and never a child have I to leave it to." I thought of the confidence trick, and resolved I would be on the alert for the vestiges of my five hundred pounds. He proceeded to enlarge on his loneliness, and the trouble he had to find a proper disposition of his money. "I have weighed this plan and that plan, charities, institutions, and scholarships, and libraries, and I have come to this conclusion at last"—he fixed his eyes on my face—"that I will find some young fellow, ambitious, pure-minded, and poor, healthy in body and healthy in mind, and, in short, make him my heir, give him all that I have." He repeated, "Give him all that I have. So that he will suddenly be lifted out of all the trouble and struggle in which his sympathies have been educated, to freedom and influence."

I tried to seem disinterested. With a transparent hypocrisy I said, "And you want my help, my professional services maybe, to find that person."

He smiled, and looked at me over his cigarette, and I laughed at his quiet exposure of my modest pretense.

"What a career such a man might have!" he said. "It fills me with envy to think how I have accumulated—that another man may spend—

"But there are conditions, of course, burdens to be imposed. He must, for instance, take my name. You cannot expect everything without some return. And I must go into all the circumstances of his life before I can accept him. He *must* be sound. I must know his heredity, how his parents and grandparents died, have the strictest inquiries made into his private morals."

This modified my secret congratulations a little.

"And do I understand," said I, "that I—"

"Yes," he said, almost fiercely. "You. *You.*"

I answered never a word. My imagination was dancing wildly, my innate skepticism was useless to modify its transports. There was not a particle of gratitude in my mind—I did not know what to say nor how to say it. "But why me in particular?" I said at last.

He had chanced to hear of me from Professor Haslar, he said, as a typically sound and sane young man, and he wished, as far as possible, to leave his money where health and integrity were assured.

That was my first meeting with the little old man. He was mysterious about himself; he would not give his name yet, he said, and after I had answered some questions of his, he left me at the Blavitiski portal. I noticed that he drew a handful of gold coins from his pocket when it came to paying for the lunch. His insistence upon bodily health was curious. In accordance with an arrangement we had made I applied that day for a life policy in the Loyal Insurance Company for a large sum, and I was exhaustively overhauled by the medical advisers of that company in the subsequent week. Even that did not satisfy him, and he insisted I must be re-examined by the great Doctor Henderson.

It was Friday in Whitsun week before he came to a decision. He called me down, quite late in the evening—nearly nine it was—from cramming chemical equations for my Preliminary Scientific examination. He was standing in the passage under the feeble gas lamp, and his face was a grotesque interplay of shadows. He seemed more bowed than when I had first seen him, and his cheeks had sunk in a little.

His voice shook with emotion. "Everything is satisfactory, Mr. Eden," he said. "Everything is quite, quite satisfactory. And this night of all nights, you must dine with me and celebrate your—accession." He was interrupted by a cough. "You won't have long to wait, either," he said, wiping his handkerchief across his lips, and gripping my hand with his long bony claw that was disengaged. "Certainly not very long to wait."

We went into the street and called a cab. I remember every incident of that drive vividly, the swift, easy motion, the vivid contrast of gas and oil and electric light, the crowds of people in the streets, the place in Regent Street to which we went, and the sumptuous dinner we were served with there. I was disconcerted at first by the well-dressed waiter's glances at my rough clothes, bothered by the stones of the olives, but as the champagne warmed my blood, my confidence revived. At first the old man talked of himself. He had already told me his name in the cab; he was Egbert Elvesham, the great philosopher, whose name I had known since I was a lad at school. It seemed incredible to me that this man, whose intelligence had so early dominated mine, this great abstraction, should suddenly realize itself as this decrepit, familiar figure. I dare say every young fellow who has suddenly fallen among celebrities has felt something of my disappointment. He told me now of the future that the feeble streams of his life would presently leave dry for me, houses, copyrights, investments; I had never suspected that philosophers were so rich. He watched me drink and eat with a touch of envy. "What a capacity for living you have!" he said; and then with a sigh, a sigh of relief I could have thought it, "It will not be long."

"Ay," said I, my head swimming now with champagne; "I have a future perhaps—of a passing agreeable sort, thanks to you. I shall now have the honor of your name. But you have a past. Such a past as is worth all my future."

He shook his head and smiled, as I thought, with half sad appreciation of my flattering admiration. "That future," he said, "would you in truth change it?" The waiter came with liqueurs. "You will not perhaps mind taking my name, taking my position, but would you indeed—willingly—take my years?"

"With your achievements," said I gallantly.

He smiled again. "Kümmel—both," he said to the waiter, and turned his attention to a little paper packet he had taken from his pocket. "This hour," said he, "this after-dinner hour is the hour of small things. Here is a scrap of my unpublished wisdom." He opened the packet with his shaking yellow fingers, and showed a little pinkish powder on the paper. "This," said he— "well, you must guess what it is. But Kümmel—put a dash of this powder in it—is Himmel."

His large grayish eyes watched mine with an inscrutable expression.

It was a bit of a shock to me to find this great teacher gave his mind to the flavor of liqueurs. However, I feigned an interest in his weakness, for I was drunk enough for such small sycophancy.

He parted the powder between the little glasses, and, rising suddenly, with a strange unexpected dignity, held out his hand towards me. I imitated his action, and the glasses rang. "To a quick succession," said he, and raised his glass towards his lips.

"Not that," I said hastily. "Not that."

The Story of the Late Mr. Elvesham

He paused with the liqueur at the level of his chin, and his eyes blazing into mine.

"To a long life," said I.

He hesitated. "To a long life," said he, with a sudden bark of laughter, and with eyes fixed on one another we tilted the little glasses. His eyes looked straight into mine, and as I drained the stuff off, I felt a curiously intense sensation. The first touch of it set my brain in a furious tumult; I seemed to feel an actual physical stirring in my skull, and a seething humming filled my ears. I did not notice the flavor in my mouth, the aroma that filled my throat; I saw only the gray intensity of his gaze that burnt into mine. The draft, the mental confusion, the noise and stirring in my head, seemed to last an interminable time. Curious vague impressions of half-forgotten things danced and vanished on the edge of my consciousness. At last he broke the spell. With a sudden explosive sigh he put down his glass.

"Well?" he said.

"It's glorious," said I, though I had not tasted the stuff.

My head was spinning. I sat down. My brain was chaos. Then my perception grew clear and minute as though I saw things in a concave mirror. His manner seemed to have changed into something nervous and hasty. He pulled out his watch and grimaced at it. "Eleven seven! And tonight I must—Seven twenty-five. Waterloo! I must go at once." He called for the bill, and struggled with his coat. Officious waiters came to our assistance. In another moment I was wishing him good-by, over the apron of a cab, and still with an absurd feeling of minute distinctness, as though—how can I express it?—I not only saw but *felt* through an inverted opera glass.

"That stuff," he said. He put his hand to his forehead. "I ought not to have given it to you. It will make your head split tomorrow. Wait a minute. Here." He handed me out a little flat thing like a Seidlitz powder. "Take that in water as you are going to bed. The other thing was a drug. Not till you're ready to go to bed, mind. It will clear your head. That's all. One more shake—Futurus!"

I gripped his shriveled claw. "Good-by," he said, and by the droop of his eyelids I judged he too was a little under the influence of that brain-twisting cordial.

He recollected something else with a start, felt in his breast pocket, and produced another packet, this time a cylinder the size and shape of a shaving stick. "Here," said he. "I'd almost forgotten. Don't open this until I come tomorrow—but take it now."

It was so heavy that I well-nigh dropped it. "All ri'!" said I, and he grinned at me through the cab window as the cabman flicked his horse into wakefulness. It was a white packet he had given me, with red seals at either end and along its edge. "If this isn't money," said I, "it's platinum or lead."

I stuck it with elaborate care into my pocket, and with a whirling brain walked home through the Regent Street loiterers and the dark back streets beyond Portland Road. I remember the sensations of that walk very vividly; strange as they were, I was still so far myself that I could notice my strange mental state, and wonder whether this stuff I had had was opium—a drug beyond my experience. It is hard now to describe the peculiarity of my mental strangeness—mental doubling vaguely

The Story of the Late Mr. Elvesham

expresses it. As I was walking up Regent Street I found in my mind a queer persuasion that it was Waterloo Station, and had an odd impulse to get into the Polytechnic as a man might get into a train. I put a knuckle in my eye, and it was Regent Street. How can I express it? You see a skillful actor looking quietly at you, he pulls a grimace, and lo!—another person. Is it too extravagant if I tell you that it seemed to me as if Regent Street had, for the moment, done that? Then, being persuaded it was Regent Street again, I was oddly muddled about some fantastic reminiscences that cropped up. "Thirty years ago," thought I, "it was here that I quarreled with my brother." Then I burst out laughing, to the astonishment and encouragement of a group of night prowlers. Thirty years ago I did not exist, and never in my life had I boasted a brother. The stuff was surely liquid folly, for the poignant regret for that lost brother still clung to me. Along Portland Road the madness took another turn. I began to recall vanished shops, and to compare the street with what it used to be. Confused, troubled thinking is comprehensible enough after the drink I had taken, but what puzzled me were these curiously vivid phantasm memories that had crept into my mind, and not only the memories that had crept in, but also the memories that had slipped out. I stopped opposite Stevens's, the natural history dealer's, and cudgeled my brains to think what he had to do with me. A bus went by, and sounded exactly like the rumbling of a train. I seemed to be dipping into some dark, remote pit for the recollection. "Of course," said I, at last, "he has promised me three frogs tomorrow. Odd I should have forgotten."

Do they still show children dissolving views? In those

I remember one view would begin like a faint ghost, and grow and oust another. In just that way it seemed to me that a ghostly set of new sensations was struggling with those of my ordinary self.

I went on through Euston Road to Tottenham Court Road, puzzled, and a little frightened, and scarcely noticed the unusual way I was taking, for commonly I used to cut through the intervening network of back streets. I turned into University Street, to discover that I had forgotten my number. Only by a strong effort did I recall 11A, and even then it seemed to me that it was a thing some forgotten person had told me. I tried to steady my mind by recalling the incidents of the dinner, and for the life of me I could conjure up no picture of my host's face; I saw him only as a shadowy outline, as one might see oneself reflected in a window through which one was looking. In his place, however, I had a curious exterior vision of myself, sitting at a table, flushed, bright-eyed, and talkative.

"I must take this other powder," said I. "This is getting impossible."

I tried the wrong side of the hall for my candle and the matches, and had a doubt of which landing my room might be on. "I'm drunk," I said, "that's certain," and blundered needlessly on the staircase to sustain the proposition.

At the first glance my room seemed unfamiliar. "What rot!" I said, and stared about me. I seemed to bring myself back by the effort, and the odd phantasmal quality passed into the concrete familiar. There was the old glass still, with my notes on the albumens stuck in the corner of the frame, my old everyday suit of clothes pitched about the floor. And yet it was not so real after all. I felt an idiotic persuasion trying to creep into my mind, as it were, that I was in a railway carriage in a train just stopping, that I was peering out of the window at some unknown station. I gripped the bedrail firmly to reassure myself. "It's clairvoyance, perhaps," I said. "I must write to the Psychical Research Society."

I put the rouleau on my dressing table, sat on my bed, and began to take off my boots. It was as if the picture of my present sensations was painted over some other picture that was trying to show through. "Curse it!" said I; "my wits are going, or am I in two places at once?" Half-undressed, I tossed the powder into a glass and drank it off. It effervesced, and became a fluorescent amber color. Before I was in bed my mind was already tranquilized. I felt the pillow at my cheek, and thereupon I must have fallen asleep.

I awoke abruptly out of a dream of strange beasts, and found myself lying on my back. Probably everyone knows that dismal, emotional dream from which one escapes, awake indeed, but strangely cowed. There was a curious taste in my mouth, a tired feeling in my limbs, a sense of cutaneous discomfort. I lay with my head motionless on my pillow, expecting that my feeling of strangeness and terror would pass away, and that I should then doze off again to sleep. But instead of that, my uncanny sensations increased. At first I could perceive nothing wrong about me. There was a faint light in the room, so faint that it was the very next thing to darkness, and the furniture stood out in it as vague blots of absolute darkness. I stared with my eyes just over the bedclothes.

It came into my mind that someone had entered the

room to rob me of my rouleau of money, but after lying for some moments, breathing regularly to simulate sleep, I realized this was mere fancy. Nevertheless, the uneasy assurance of something wrong kept fast hold of me. With an effort I raised my head from the pillow, and peered about me at the dark. What it was I could not conceive. I looked at the dim shapes around me, the greater and lesser darknesses that indicated curtains, table, fireplace, bookshelves, and so forth. Then I began to perceive something unfamiliar in the forms of the darkness. Had the bed turned round? Yonder should be the bookshelves, and something shrouded and pallid rose there, something that would not answer to the bookshelves, however I looked at it. It was far too big to be my shirt thrown on a chair.

Overcoming a childish terror, I threw back the bedclothes and thrust my leg out of bed. Instead of coming out of my trucklebed upon the floor, I found my foot scarcely reached the edge of the mattress. I made another step, as it were, and sat up on the edge of the bed. By the side of my bed should be the candle, and the matches upon the broken chair. I put out my hand and touched—nothing. I waved my hand in the darkness, and it came against some heavy hanging, soft and thick in texture, which gave a rustling noise at my touch. I grasped this and pulled it; it appeared to be a curtain suspended over the head of my bed.

I was now thoroughly awake, and beginning to realize that I was in a strange room. I was puzzled. I tried to recall the overnight circumstances, and I found them now, curiously enough, vivid in my memory; the supper, my reception of the little packages, my wonder whether I was intoxicated, my slow undressing, the coolness to my flushed face of my pillow. I felt a sudden distrust. Was that last night, or the night before? At any rate, this room was strange to me, and I could not imagine how I had got into it. The dim, pallid outline was growing paler, and I perceived it was a window, with the dark shape of an oval toilet-glass against the weak intimation of the dawn that filtered through the blind. I stood up, and was surprised by a curious feeling of weakness and unsteadiness. With trembling hands outstretched, I walked slowly towards the window, getting, nevertheless, a bruise on the knee from a chair by the way. I fumbled round the glass, which was large, with handsome brass sconces, to find the blind-cord. I could not find any. By chance I took hold of the tassel, and with the click of a spring the blind ran up.

I found myself looking out upon a scene that was altogether strange to me. The night was overcast, and through the flocculent gray of the heaped clouds there filtered a faint half-light of dawn. Just at the edge of the sky the cloud-canopy had a blood-red rim. Below, everything was dark and indistinct, dim hills in the distance, a vague mass of buildings running up into pinnacles, trees like spilt ink, and below the window a tracery of black bushes and pale gray paths. It was so unfamiliar that for the moment I thought myself still dreaming. I felt the toilet table; it appeared to be made of some polished wood, and was rather elaborately furnished—there were little cut-glass bottles and a brush upon it. There was also a queer little object, horseshoe-shape it felt, with smooth, hard projections, lying in a saucer. I could find no matches nor candlestick.

I turned my eyes to the room again. Now the blind was up, faint specters of its furnishing came out of the darkness. There was a huge curtained bed, and the fireplace at its foot had a large white mantel with something of the shimmer of marble.

I leaned against the toilet-table, shut my eyes and opened them again, and tried to think. The whole thing was far too real for dreaming. I was inclined to imagine there was still some hiatus in my memory, as a consequence of my draft of that strange liqueur; that I had come into my inheritance perhaps, and suddenly lost my recollection of everything since my good fortune had been announced. Perhaps, if I waited a little, things would be clearer to me again. Yet my dinner with old Elvesham was now singularly vivid and recent. The champagne, the observant waiters, the powder, and the liqueurs—I could have staked my soul it all happened a few hours ago.

And then occurred a thing so trivial and yet so terrible to me that I shiver now to think of that moment. I spoke aloud. I said, "How the devil did I get here?" . . . *And the voice was not my own.*

It was not my own, it was thin, the articulation was slurred, the resonance of my facial bones was different. Then, to reassure myself, I ran one hand over the other, and felt loose folds of skin, the bony laxity of age. "Surely," I said, in that horrible voice that had somehow established itself in my throat, "surely this thing is a dream!" Almost as quickly as if I did it involuntarily, I thrust my fingers into my mouth. My teeth had gone. My fingertips ran on the flaccid surface of an even row of shriveled gums. I was sick with dismay and disgust.

I felt then a passionate desire to see myself, to realize at once in its full horror the ghastly change that had come upon me. I tottered to the mantel, and felt along

The Story of the Late Mr. Elvesham

it for matches. As I did so, a barking cough sprang up in my throat, and I clutched the thick flannel nightdress I found about me. There were no matches there, and I suddenly realized that my extremities were cold. Sniffing and coughing, whimpering a little, perhaps, I fumbled back to bed. "It is surely a dream," I whispered to myself as I clambered back, "surely a dream." It was a senile repetition. I pulled the bedclothes over my shoulders, over my ears, I thrust my withered hand under the pillow, and determined to compose myself to sleep. Of course it was a dream. In the morning the dream would be over, and I should wake up strong and vigorous again to my youth and studies. I shut my eyes, breathed regularly, and, finding myself wakeful, began to count slowly through the powers of three.

But the thing I desired would not come. I could not get to sleep. And the persuasion of the inexorable reality of the change that had happened to me grew steadily. Presently I found myself with my eyes wide open, the powers of three forgotten, and my skinny fingers upon my shriveled gums. I was, indeed, suddenly and abruptly, an old man. I had in some unaccountable manner fallen through my life and come to old age, in some way I had been cheated of all the best of my life, of love, of struggle, of strength, and hope. I groveled into the pillow and tried to persuade myself that such hallucination was possible. Imperceptibly, steadily, the dawn grew clearer.

At last, despairing of further sleep, I sat up in bed and looked about me. A chill twilight rendered the whole chamber visible. It was spacious and well-furnished, better furnished than any room I had ever slept in before. A candle and matches became dimly visible upon a little pedestal in a recess. I threw back the bedclothes, and, shivering with the rawness of the early morning, albeit it was summertime, I got out and lit the candle. Then, trembling horribly, so that the extinguisher rattled on its spike—I tottered to the glass and saw—*Elvesham's face!* It was nonetheless horrible because I had already dimly feared as much. He had already seemed physically weak and pitiful to me, but seen now, dressed only in a coarse flannel nightdress, that fell apart and showed the stringy neck, seen now as my own body, I cannot describe its desolate decrepitude. The hollow cheeks, the straggling tail of dirty gray hair, the rheumy, bleared eyes, the quivering, shriveled lips, the lower displaying a gleam of the pink interior lining, and those horrible dark gums showing. You who are mind and body together, at your natural years, cannot imagine what this fiendish imprisonment meant to me. To be young and full of the desire and energy of youth, and to be caught, and presently to be crushed in this tottering ruin of a body....

But I wander from the course of my story. For some time I must have been stunned at this change that had come upon me. It was daylight when I did so far gather myself together as to think. In some inexplicable way I had been changed, though how, short of magic, the thing had been done, I could not say. And as I thought, the diabolical ingenuity of Elvesham came home to me. It seemed plain to me that as I found myself in his, so he must be in possession of *my* body, of my strength, that is, and my future. But how to prove it? Then, as I thought, the thing became so incredible, even to me, that my mind reeled, and I had to pinch myself, to feel my toothless gums, to see myself in the glass, and touch

The Story of the Late Mr. Elvesham

the things about me, before I could steady myself to face the facts again. Was all life hallucination? Was I indeed Elvesham, and he me? Had I been dreaming of Eden overnight? Was there any Eden? But if I was Elvesham, I should remember where I was on the previous morning, the name of the town in which I lived, what happened before the dream began. I struggled with my thoughts. I recalled the queer doubleness of my memories overnight. But now my mind was clear. Not the ghost of any memories but those proper to Eden could I raise.

"This way lies insanity!" I cried in my piping voice. I staggered to my feet, dragged my feeble, heavy limbs to the washhand-stand, and plunged my gray head into a basin of cold water. Then, toweling myself, I tried again. It was no good. I felt beyond all question that I was indeed Eden, not Elvesham. But Eden in Elvesham's body!

Had I been a man of any other age, I might have given myself up to my fate as one enchanted. But in these skeptical days miracles do not pass current. Here was some trick of psychology. What a drug and a steady stare could do, a drug and a steady stare, or some similar treatment, could surely undo. Men have lost their memories before. But to exchange memories as one does umbrellas! I laughed. Alas! not a healthy laugh, but a wheezing, senile titter. I could have fancied old Elvesham laughing at my plight, and a gust of petulant anger, unusual to me, swept across my feelings. I began dressing eagerly in the clothes I found lying about on the floor, and only realized when I was dressed that it was an evening suit I had assumed. I opened the wardrobe and found some more ordinary clothes, a pair of plaid trousers, and an old-fashioned dressing gown. I put a venerable smoking cap on my venerable head, and, coughing a little from my exertions, tottered out upon the landing.

It was then, perhaps, a quarter to six, and the blinds were closely drawn and the house quite silent. The landing was a spacious one, a broad, richly carpeted staircase went down into the darkness of the hall below, and before me a door ajar showed me a writing desk, a revolving bookcase, the back of a study chair, and a fine array of bound books, shelf upon shelf.

"My study," I mumbled, and walked across the landing. Then at the sound of my voice a thought struck me, and I went back to the bedroom and put in the set of false teeth. They slipped in with the ease of old habit. "That's better," said I, gnashing them, and so returned to the study.

The drawers of the writing desk were locked. Its revolving top was also locked. I could see no indications of the keys and there were none in the pocket of my trousers. I shuffled back at once to the bedroom, and went through the dress suit, and afterwards the pockets of all the garments I could find. I was very eager, and one might have imagined that burglars had been at work, to see my room when I had done. Not only were there no keys to be found, but not a coin, nor a scrap of paper—save only the receipted bill of the overnight dinner.

A curious weariness asserted itself. I sat down and stared at the garments flung here and there, their pockets turned inside out. My first frenzy had already flickered out. Every moment I was beginning to realize the immense intelligence of the plans of my enemy, to see more and more clearly the hopelessness of my position. With an effort I rose and hurried hobbling into the study again. On the staircase was a housemaid pulling up the blinds. She stared, I think, at the expression of my face. I shut the door of the study behind me, and, seizing a poker, began an attack upon the desk. That is how they found me. The cover of the desk was split, the lock smashed, the letters torn out of the pigeonholes and tossed about the room. In my senile rage I had flung about the pens and other such light stationery, and overturned the ink. Moreover, a large vase upon the mantel had got broken—I do not know how. I could find no checkbook, no money, no indications of the slightest use for the recovery of my body. I was battering madly at the drawers, when the butler, backed by two woman servants, intruded upon me.

That simply is the story of my change. No one will believe my frantic assertions. I am treated as one demented, and even at this moment I am under restraint. But I am sane, absolutely sane, and to prove it I have sat down to write this story minutely as the things happened to me. I appeal to the reader, whether there is any trace of insanity in the style or method of the story he has been reading. I am a young man locked away in an old man's body. But the clear fact is incredible to everyone. Naturally I appear demented to those who will not believe this, naturally I do not know the names of my secretaries, of the doctors who come to see me, of my servants and neighbors, of this town (wherever it is) where I find myself. Naturally I lose myself in my own house, and suffer inconveniences of every sort. Naturally I ask the oddest questions. Naturally I weep and cry out, and have paroxysms of despair. I have no money and no checkbook. The bank will not recognize my signature, for I suppose that, allowing for the feeble muscles I now have, my handwriting is still Eden's. These people about me will not let me go to the bank personally. It seems, indeed, that there is no bank in this town, and that I have an account in some part of London. It seems that Elvesham kept the name of his solicitor secret from all his household. I can ascertain nothing. Elvesham was, of course, a profound student of mental science, and all my declarations of the facts of the case merely confirm the theory that my insanity is the outcome of overmuch brooding upon psychology. Dreams of the personal identity indeed! Two days ago I was a healthy youngster, with all life before me; now I am a furious old man, unkempt, and desperate, and miserable, prowling about a great, luxurious, strange house, watched, feared, and avoided as a lunatic by everyone about me. And in London is Elvesham beginning life again in a vigorous body, and with all the accumulated knowledge and wisdom of threescore and ten. He has stolen my life.

What has happened I do not clearly know. In the study are volumes of manuscript notes referring chiefly to the psychology of memory, and parts of what may be either calculations or ciphers in symbols absolutely strange to me. In some passages there are indications that he was also occupied with the philosophy of mathematics. I take it he has transferred the whole of his memories, the accumulation that makes up his personality, from this old withered brain of his to mine, and, similarly, that he has transferred mine to his discarded tenement. Practically, that is, he has changed bodies. But how such a change may be possible is without the

The Story of the Late Mr. Elvesham

range of my philosophy. I have been a materialist for all my thinking life, but here, suddenly, is a clear case of man's detachability from matter.

One desperate experiment I am about to try. I sit writing here before putting the matter to issue. This morning, with the help of a table knife that I had secreted at breakfast, I succeeded in breaking open a fairly obvious secret drawer in this wrecked writing desk. I discovered nothing save a little green glass phial containing a white powder. Round the neck of the phial was a label, and thereon was written this one word, "*Release.*" This may be—is most probably—poison. I can understand Elvesham placing poison in my way, and I should be sure that it was his intention so to get rid of the only living witness against him, were it not for this careful concealment. The man has practically solved the problem of immortality. Save for the spite of chance, he will live in my body until it has aged, and then, again, throwing it aside, he will assume some other victim's youth and strength. When one remembers his heartlessness, it is terrible to think of the ever-growing experience that . . . How long has he been leaping from body to body? . . . But I tire of writing. The powder appears to be soluble in water. The taste is not unpleasant.

There the narrative found upon Mr. Elvesham's desk ends. His dead body lay between the desk and the chair. The latter had been pushed back, probably by his last convulsions. The story was written in pencil, and in a crazy hand, quite unlike his usual minute characters. There remain only two curious facts to record. Indisputably there was some connection between Eden and Elvesham, since the whole of Elvesham's property was bequeathed to the young man. But he never inherited. When Elvesham committed suicide, Eden was, strangely enough, already dead. Twenty-four hours before, he had been knocked down by a cab and killed instantly, at the crowded crossing at the intersection of Gower Street and Euston Road. So that the only human being who could have thrown light upon this fantastic narrative is beyond the reach of questions. Without further comment, I leave this extraordinary matter to the reader's individual judgment.

The Strange Occurrences Connected with Captain John Russell

by Neil Bell

When John Russell disappeared, the villagers said the devil had taken him.

John Russell was born on January 14th, 1832, at Covehithe, a small village on the Suffolk coast some nine miles south of Lowestoft. His father, Edward Russell, farmed a piece of land there of about ten acres and from this sandy soil, so close to the sea that it was little more fertile than a salting, he scratched a meager living. He had built the house himself with only his wife to help and Spurr Farm (it was no more than a four-roomed thatched cottage) had a queer look about it. The villagers found it difficult to say what there was queer about it, but that it did look queer there wasn't any doubt: it looked in fact, not quite "all there." It was not because it had been built by a man who brought untaught hands to the job, for it was by no means uncommon in those parts for a man to build his own house, be he farmer or fisherman: that was not the reason at all: in fact, there was no reason about it.

Spurr Farm *looked* queer; it could not be gainsaid and that was all that anybody could say.

There was no one to help at the farm; neither to help Jess Russell in the house and with her hens nor Edward in the fields and with his six cows; they couldn't afford the wages. It was all they could do working from dawn to sunset all the year round to scrape a living for the two of them. There was never a holiday in their lives; never even a day or half day off. They were a devout couple but Covehithe Church (itself queer, being built on to the inside wall of the former large church, then in ruins) had seen them but once worshiping together (the day they were married). Henceforward one went to the Sunday morning service, the other to the evening; and not infrequently, to their great distress, neither would be able to go owing to a cow calving or some other unusual circumstance: and at these times they would spend longer upon their knees in prayer at bedtime, and so tired out were they that more than once Edward, the weaker vessel, would fall asleep on his knees.

It was into this devout, hardworking and pinched little household that John Russell was born towards the end of that black period after Waterloo when bad harvests, added to the nation's impoverishment from the long war, had strewed the countryside with starving beggars and filled the big towns with jobless men who either sank into a grey hopeless apathy and with their wives and children entered the workhouses, or, becoming bitter and desperate, turned to robbery and murder and found their way in thousands to the gallows, the prisons, or the hulks to await transportation for life.

John was apparently a very ordinary and quite normal little boy up to the time he was thirteen, for nothing is known about him until then. He probably went to the village school, or he may have been taught by one of his parents; certainly he could read and write and figure, for he was one day to hold a master's ticket in the Merchant Navy and to be captain of more than one sizable ship; the *Jane Gorley*, for example, being a fine brig of five hundred tons burthen.

John was not many months past his thirteenth birthday and within a few weeks of his confirmation (a perhaps significant fact) when the most extraordinary things began to happen at Spurr Farm. One morning when Edward Russell was working in the smaller of his two fields, his wife in the house, and John in the garden, a shower of stones fell on the house, many hitting the chimney stacks and bounding off, and others pouring down straight into the garden or on to the small pebbled yard. There were scores of them, the sort of various-sized pebbles that made up the beach at Covehithe.

From that day onwards for months, with occasional breaks of a few days or sometimes even a week, unexplainable things continued to happen at the farm. Showers of stones were frequent and more than once they came through the windows and covered the floors; plates, dishes, crocks, and table cutlery moved, rattled and danced on shelves or threw themselves across rooms; tables jumped; chairs turned themselves upside down; beds rocked and swayed like boats in a rough sea. John was out in the garden one morning when some clothes were hanging on the line; suddenly a sheet burst into flames and was consumed. At another time in the kitchen, he suddenly cried out "Look!" and pointed to the curtain which was seen to be on fire.

Edward Russell and his wife were naturally enough concerned about these things, but they do not appear to have been frightened and perhaps of all the village they were the least perturbed. The extraordinary events were discussed over and over in the two village ale houses, and news of them reached adjacent towns and villages, so that curious sightseers came from Southwold, Kessingland, Pakefield and even from as far as Lowestoft, to stand and stare at the farm and to hope that something would happen while they were there.

The most accepted view in the neighborhood was that the farm was in the possession of evil spirits and the vicar of Covehithe, the Rev. Charles Rayner, after poohpoohing the idea, was finally persuaded to visit the farm and read the services of Exorcism. But the phenomena continued, and indeed, with increasing and now dangerous violence, for Mrs. Russell was struck on the head by a flying cup and her husband was slightly burnt when a settle on which he was sitting suddenly burst into flames.

And now it began to be said, in the sudden furtive way these things are said or whispered, that the boy John was at the bottom of it all; and soon it was no longer whispered but said so openly that it came to the Russells' ears, including John's. Possibly Edward and Jess Russell had long suspected that John was responsible, and now, fortified by this apparently general opinion, they taxed him with it, and at first were met with vehement denials and a flood of tears. But later, under persistent catechism, John confessed; or at least he made a statement that was accepted as a confession. Yet all his "confession" amounted to was that he had a feeling that he was the cause of these extraordinary happenings, but that he did not actually do them or know how they were done. Consulted about the confession, the vicar suggested the boy should be sent away for a holiday, and he went to some relatives named Johnson at Southwold; and there he stayed four months.

During the time he was at Southwold nothing out of the ordinary happened at Spurr Farm, but within a week of his return the manifestations began again: showers of stones; flights of utensils; dancing chairs and tables; and spontaneously igniting fabrics. The thing now began to prey upon the boy's mind and his distress was made the greater by the tale which went about the village (and quickly came to his ears) that it was not the farm which was possessed by evil spirits but he himself. The smaller children began to avoid him; the bigger ones to call after him; and the adults to eye him askance or avert their faces when he passed lest he might have the evil eye as well as be possessed by the devil; for it was soon the devil himself who possessed him and no supernumerary demon.

The upshot of this persecution was the usual one; John Russell disappeared. The villagers said the devil had taken him and one fertile liar claimed to have seen "a shape" rushing up into the sky, leaving behind it a sulphurous stink. Mr. and Mrs. Russell thought he had gone to the Johnsons, where he had been very happy. Actually, he had followed the traditional course of the unhappy or discontented boy—he had run away to sea; walked to Lowestoft and shipped as boy on one of the small vessels (of from a hundred to three hundred tons) which in those days carried cargoes to all parts of the world from a score of little ports along the east coast of England.

It was four years before he returned to Covehithe, eighteen years of age, a tall, broad fellow whom four years of as rough, hard and perilous a life as is known to mankind had certainly made a man of; a being very different from the scared nervous shrinking boy who had fled from the village to escape the pointing fingers, the suspicious eyes, the venomous tongues.

The villagers were intensely interested and excited over his return; would there now be, it was everywhere debated, a return of the manifestations? It was hoped so (if half fearfully), for life in Covehithe tended to be monotonous and no one could forget the wonderful excitement of those events of four years ago at Spurr Farm and all the enjoyable gossip they had engendered. But to the general disappointment, nothing happened; not so much as a single stone fell, nor was there a crock broken at the farm except in the way of ordinary accident. Yet John Russell's return was not without its food for gossip, for he had seen the most extraordinary things during those four years in foreign parts and he was (after a time of reciprocal readjustments) quite willing to talk about them at one or the other of the two ale houses where he regularly spent his evenings, for he had come home with a pocket full of savings and an openhandedness for which, behind his back, he was called a "dom fule" by those who took most advantage of it.

Queer tales he had indeed to tell. There was his Spanish story. His ship had put in at Valencia for a week and he and a crony, a youngster named Waters, had hired ponies and ridden to Liria about ten miles inland. There was a violent thunderstorm while they were there with torrents of rain, and with the rain fell small frogs, not in dozens or scores but in thousands, so that the roads, lanes and fields were littered with them. Neither John Russell nor Waters could speak a word of Spanish and none of the natives knew any English, so that it was impossible to get any information about this extraordinary affair; but as the natives appeared as astonished as they were, they assumed that such a miraculous shower had not occurred there previously.

This was by no means the only experience of the unaccountable falling of objects from the sky which John Russell had had during his four years at sea. During another voyage while on a visit to Sarno near Naples, he had witnessed a fall of caterpillars from a cloudless sky. They had fallen in thousands, pale green in color and about an inch and a half long; in some of the narrow lanes they were almost ankle-deep and their bodies when crushed underfoot or by the wheels of carts gave off a most nauseating smell.

Then there was the fall of hundreds of fish of all sizes from three to seven inches in length at Alvaredo in Mexico. These also fell from a cloudless sky and while many were alive and most were quite fresh, although dead, not a few were old and stinking.

Again, about a year later, when he was at Puerto Cabezas in Nicaragua, he had seen blood fall from the sky in torrents following a shower of rain. The blood fell over a very restricted area—less than an acre—and there was no doubt about its being blood, Russell said, for the local doctor, who spoke English, had collected some of the liquid, tested it, and declared it to be blood, and probably horse's.

But the sky had held other things besides inexplicable

showers for John Russell; and not for him only, for he declared that all that he had seen had been seen by many other people, in some cases by hundreds. There was, for example, the city in the sky over Jibacoa in Cuba. It was a large city, he said, larger than Norwich (to which he had apparently paid a visit during his early childhood) and seemed to be about a mile up in the sky. Everything in that "heavenly" city was perfectly clear to the innumerable eyes watching it in Jibacoa; streets, houses, churches, shops, and certain movements in the streets, but whether of people or traffic it was too distant to see. The people of Jibacoa told him that this was no new visitant to their sky, but had been seen half a dozen times in the past ten years and was supposed to be the mirage of a city hundreds, perhaps thousands, of miles away; but no one knew what city it was, although there had been many claims put in for various cities of both the old and new worlds, claims which had not however survived the interrogation of people familiar with the appearance of the suggested cities.

While, during another voyage, his ship was off Florida and he was taking his turn at the wheel just before dawn, he had seen in the lightening sky an air vessel (so he described it) traveling swiftly high overhead with a great whirring noise and showing many bright lights. His shouts brought the mate and two other members of the crew hurrying to him and the four of them, dumbstricken with wonder, watched the amazing spectacle for nearly ten minutes, when it finally disappeared.

And there was a sea serpent. It was while they were off Watling Island in the Bahamas. It was broad daylight and there was a hot sun with but a slight wind (three on the Beaufort scale, Russell said) and hardly any sea. Suddenly about half a mile astern and on the port side, there reared up out of the water a colossal head supported by a rather slender neck. The creature appeared to be pursuing them, overtook them in less than a minute, but swerved aside and passed them on the starboard side less than half a cable's length away, going as fast as a train and raising a wash which swept them from stem to stern. All who saw the serpent were agreed, Russell said, that its head was "as large as a tun," that its neck was the thickness of a horse's body, and that its length, judging from the flurry of water furthest from its head, must have been two hundred feet.

To all these stories the habitués of Covehithe's two ale houses lent an interested ear (as did their wives in turn); but they were not impressed; all these marvels had happened (or rather were said to have happened) at outlandish foreign places they'd never heard of and didn't believe existed. Even when John Russell brought maps along and showed them the places it made no difference; the places were just names on maps and they could not visualize and realize them as towns and cities and villages where lived people very like themselves. They did not, in fact, believe the tales; he'd always been a queer 'un had John Russell; look at the things that had happened at the farm. But they listened with interest; they were "good cuffers," these daft tales of John Russell's, whatever else they might be. But presently, and before John began to tire of telling and retelling his tales, they began to tire of hearing them and were soon, behind his back, jeering at him and mocking him. And after a while, when all his money was gone, it was not completely behind his back, although such was his size and strength (and their doubts about his temper) that there was no open derision; nothing more to his face than yawns and the most perfunctory attention.

Perhaps trouble might have blown up as yawns grew wider and more overt (and barely hiding grins), especially as the old lavish openhandedness was perforce a thing of the past. But there was no explosion. On a moonlit night (October 12th, 1851) John left the Lower House (the two taverns being known as the Upper House and the Lower House) at half past nine and, as he often did, set off to stroll along the beach towards Southwold before returning home. He was perfectly sober, for his purse was now so slender that he had to limit his drinking to two pints a night. He was alone, and was last seen striding across the saltings by the Preventive Officer, who was standing at his cottage door smoking his pipe. It was just over a year before he was seen again; thirteen months and three days, in fact, for he returned to Covehithe on November 15th, 1852.

Contrary to the general belief in the village, he had not been to sea again. He had a far stranger story to tell and he told this incredible tale simply and in as matter-of-fact a fashion as if he had been relating an event no more out of the ordinary than a stroll along the shore to Southwold. He said he had been living for the past year in a country in the sky. He had no recollection of how he got there, although he remembered that about halfway on his stroll to Southwold that October night in the previous year he had heard a sudden rushing noise behind him in the air and the next moment he had felt himself snatched up and borne aloft, and so rapidly that he lost consciousness. The next thing he remembered was being in a strange city in a strange country, where everything was very much like conditions on the earth but yet not quite like; there was a difference. Asked about this difference, he was vague and uncertain but repeated that there *was* a difference.

The villagers looked upon the tale as just a silly hoax at first, but as time went on and he persisted in his story, not pushing this "fantastic squit" on to them but merely answering patiently whatever questions were put to him, the hoax idea became less tenable and the village divided itself into those who held that John Russell was mad and those who thought he had had an accident, probably injuring his brain, and was suffering from loss of memory. But some of them continued to question him about this country of his in the sky. He said he did not know its name and as far as he knew it had no name. But he admitted he did not know very much about it, except the little he had seen himself; for so difficult was the language, and so utterly unlike any human language, that he had been able to learn only the merest rudiments of it during the time he was there. He said this country was not very many miles from the earth's surface, he "reckoned about forty or fifty," but he could not offer any explanation as to why it could not be seen. Its inhabitants were, he said, like human beings and yet not entirely like, and here again he became vague. Describing their attitude towards him he said it was kind but as if he were an intelligent animal rather than a being like themselves. Asked to give an example of their speech, he refused at first, saying he spoke it so badly, but being pressed he uttered a series of such grotesque noises that his listeners were convulsed with laughter, and this so offended him that he could not be persuaded to repeat his performance, and indeed for some days showed resentment at any questions about this country in the sky; and the expression of his face and his whole attitude were so minatory that the more nervous of the villagers began to suggest that if he were not so already he might very soon become a danger to the community and that it might be as well to "see parson" with a view to having John Russell put away. But nothing was done, and after a while he became once again approachable on the subject and indeed went so far as to volunteer certain of his own private opinions about that skyey country; that, for example, it was from there that came those unexplained showers of stones, frogs, fish, blood and other things which he and many others had seen fall upon the earth; that the city in the sky seen over the Cuban city of Jibacoa was no mirage but one of the cities of that country above the earth; and that the air vessel he and the mate had seen and heard in the sky near Florida had sailed from that country or from another similar country, for, he said, that he understood from the beings in the land where he had stayed a year that there were other aerial lands besides; and not only a few. Asked what his employment had been there he said that he had worked in the public gardens, and then he made the astonishing statement that he was not the only person from the earth up there but that there were quite a number, men and women. He had met but one, a man, who spoke no language he knew and seemed, he said, an imbecile, but he had learned about the others after he had become sufficiently familiar with the difficult language of the country to understand a little of what was being said. "I don't mean said to me," he explained, "for the people did not address themselves to me except in the way that we talk to domestic animals." When he was asked how he got back to the earth, he said he did not know, but that one morning he "walked into a fog" (that was his phrase) and when he came out of it he found himself in Liverpool working at the docks, and with no idea at all how he had got there.

This seemed rather a silly, not to say sorry, end to the affair and did something to revive the old hoax explanation, although the majority of the villagers were now inclined to the theory of mental derangement, with a sturdy few standing out boldly (but not to Russell's face) for the whole thing being just another of John's "dom fule" lies. However, the vicar had a word to say about the "silly and sorry" end to the story, declaring that finding oneself unaccountably in a distant town after a lapse of time which could not reasonably or coherently be accounted for was not uncommon and was due to some brain lesion which gave rise to a condition known as amnesia. Covehithe heard the vicar out with grave and polite attention, but without altering its own opinion which remained about equally divided between John Russell's being a gifted liar or just plain daft. They seemed to have forgotten the queer things that had happened on Spurr Farm during John's boyhood. But while interest in their extraordinary and vaguely perturbing fellow villager soon began to wane there were few who did not wonder what he would be up to next. They had not long to wait; within a year of his return he again disappeared. And this time he was away ten years and came back to a village that remembered him well enough (how could they forget him!) but scarcely recognized in the brown-bearded, middle-aged (as he seemed) Captain John Russell of the brig *Jane Gorley* (berthed at Lowestoft quay) the moody and rather frightening young man who had lived among them all his life and twice so suddenly vanished.

There was, to the relief of the villagers, nothing moody or frightening about Captain John Russell, who seemed just a big bluff hearty seaman, a type they were familiar with and with whom they could be completely at ease, without any rather unpleasant reservations—uncanny reservations. Nor had he brought back with him this time any fantastic tales about countries in the sky; nor indeed tales about anything else, to judge by his reserve during the first few months of his return. It was no morose taciturnity, for he made no secret that he had spent the past ten years at sea and having obtained his master's ticket had captained three fine ships, the *Jane Gorley* being the last. And it was to be the last, for his mother and father having both died, and Spurr Farm and the ten acres now being his, he declared his intention of leaving the sea and settling down to the farming life. "And take a wife," the gossips added to themselves; and a number of the younger women began without delay to set their caps at him, keeping well in the backs of their minds his queer past and his rather uncomfortable reputation, thus exemplifying the local saying that a woman would risk marrying the devil rather than remain unwed.

But Captain John Russell did not take a wife. He took on a hand to help him on the farm, a young man named

Tom Hurr, and the rest he did for himself, not only the cooking and cleaning but his own washing; no great or unusual feat after all for a merchant seaman.

After a while an even less pleasant side of him began to emerge, or rather re-emerge. He began to abandon his reserve and to talk about his strange adventures and his stranger ideas. The new railway which had come to Suffolk was in a way to blame, for it brought visitors from the big cities to the coast towns and some of these visitors found their way to Covehithe and into the Upper and Lower Houses where, at one or the other, regularly each evening, Captain John Russell was to be found from nine until ten o'clock playing cribbage and drinking his two pints of beer. It was never more than two pints when he was paying for it himself, but quite frequently a visitor, perhaps struck and attracted by his appearance (for he was a fine-looking man) and it may be by something a trifle peculiar in that appearance, would enter into conversation with him and offer him a drink, several drinks, frequently by no means a few. And it was then that under the genial influence of the good beer of those days, or perhaps his vanity briefly caressed by the notice taken of him, he began to tell again of the astonishing sights he had seen, and was soon launched upon the tale of his year's sojourn in the country above the earth. And now he was wont to embroider the tale; or perhaps during the past ten years forgotten things had come back to him; or by long pondering during watches things had been elucidated which had hitherto been dark. For he now began to put forward the most grotesque theories about the solar system and to declare that these things had been told him by the superior things inhabiting the country in the sky. He said that the earth was not round but pear-shaped, and that far from rotating on its axis and hurtling through space at eighteen miles a second (or something over sixty thousand miles an hour) it was stationary, utterly motionless; that it did not revolve round the sun, that body making a circuit of the earth, as did the moon; that the relative distances between the bodies making up our solar system as given by orthodox earthly astronomers were ludicrously exaggerated, the sun in fact being distant no more than a few thousand miles; the moon a mere hundred; and the planets certainly no more than a thousand. And as if this were not enough he declared that neither gravitation nor attraction nor the motion of light had any existence outside the crazy brains of our earth scientists; and finally, that all the planets of our system, together with many "countries in the sky" (invisible to us for some reason he could not explain) were inhabited by beings very like ourselves, some inferior, some vastly superior, and that not only had they been signaling to the earth for very many years, but some of their inhabitants had paid visits to the earth and others had traveled here by air vessels to reconnoiter the earth and occasionally to kidnap some of its dwellers, as he had been kidnapped on the shore between Covehithe and Southwold.

The summer visitors to Covehithe were naturally considerably interested and greatly amused by these queer tales and grotesque theories, some being so unmannerly as to make no attempt to hide their amusement and indeed make it boorishly vocal. This behavior abruptly cut short their entertainment, the Captain refusing to be drawn any more either by liquor or blandishments and if pressed began to display such temper and to assume so menacing an air that even the most ill-bred of these summer birds of passage learned discretion, if not better manners. He did indeed, finally, to escape their ill-bred importunities, cease to frequent the two Houses, foregoing his cribbage and his nightly refreshment, to avoid what he clearly looked upon as the grossest of insults. And presently this avoidance of the ale houses during the summer months grew into a general avoidance most of the year and finally altogether; and by the time he had been home from the sea a lustrum he passed his evenings, after his work was done, either at home reading or woodcarving (for which he had a great gift), or taking walks along the beach usually to Southwold; but on not infrequent occasions he would go as far afield as Lowestoft, returning in the small hours of the morning. But however late he went to bed he was up as early as any other farmer in the county and about his duties before Tom Hurr arrived.

And then things began to happen at the farm again. There were first similar showers of stones to those which had fallen when John Russell was a boy of thirteen. They fell on the house, on his fields (an especially heavy shower coming down on what was known as Windy Corner), they hit and rebounded off the chimney stacks, and they came in at the windows. Captain John Russell took no notice of the phenomena and Tom Hurr was equally unperturbed, but in Tom's case it was only an appearance of unconcern. Some of the features of the former visitations were lacking: there were no movements in the house of utensils and furniture and no instance of burning; but outside the house there were manifestations which had not previously occurred. One hot afternoon (it was July 15th, 1866) the sky became overcast above Covehithe and there fell such a hot stillness of the air that wild birds and domestic birds and beasts were affected and showed signs of uneasiness and fear. Tom Hurr was bringing in the cows for milking and Captain Russell was working in the garden, when suddenly a ball of fire rushed through the air towards the house; there was a flash, a loud explosion and an all-pervading stink of sulphur. Near where Russell had been working the earth was thrown up, and digging into the hole he brought up a roughly globular lump of metal about the size of a coconut, which the curator of Norwich City Museum (where it and some of the other objects which fell at Spurr Farm may be seen) declared was not of meteoric origin. There was no rainfall at the time of this "thunderbolt" (as the villagers called it) and shortly after its fall the sky cleared and a freshening breeze sprang up. Three weeks later a flat stone object fell from a clear sky onto Spurr Farm. It struck the chimney stack, chipping off pieces of the brickwork, and rebounded into the garden where Tom Hurr was standing. It was a flat piece of stone ten inches by seven by one and weighed two and a half pounds. It had been chipped, or worked, or knapped, and geologists who later examined it declared it to be a worked stone axhead similar to those made in England in the Stone Age.

During the next few years over a score of these "axheads" fell on or near the farm, one falling so obliquely that it crashed through a window and smashed crockery on a table. At night, lights were seen in the sky above the farm on many occasions, and on two (the nights of April 5th, 1866 and September 21st, 1867) something was seen in the sky directly over the farm and about half a mile up; it was flashing a light and from it came a whirring noise. Those who saw it (and they were most of the adults of Covehithe) declared it was an air vessel. It hovered over the farm for nearly half an hour and then drove away seawards at great speed, ascending rapidly.

These things were greatly disturbing the mind of Tom Hurr and many times he decided to leave Captain John Russell's service but always he changed his mind, for Russell was an easy master and the pay was better than he could get elsewhere. And then, in the morning of October 3rd, 1868, Tom Hurr was plowing at Windy Corner when out of a clear sky a piece of rock hurtled down, narrowly missed him, plunged into the earth, scattering soil over him and terrifying the two horses. If Hurr were not actually terrified he was decidedly shaken and within a week he had left Spurr Farm and left not only the farm but Covehithe too, as if he could not put too great a distance between himself and the place where such disturbing things were happening. The piece of rock when dug up was found to be an irregular shaped lump of quartz as large as a football and weighing twelve pounds, six ounces.

No one came to the farm to replace Tom Hurr and thenceforward Captain John Russell held no intercourse with the villagers; what shopping he did, and it was not much, was done in Southwold. Except at his work he was never seen, apart from occasional glimpses caught of him going or returning from one of his frequent nightly walks along the shore, north or south.

It was now believed by everyone in Covehithe that he

was mad although quite harmless. As for Spurr Farm, people began to give it a wide berth, even by day, and at night no one could have gone near it.

We now come to the final event in the long chain of strange happenings connected with the life of Captain John Russell. It was on the night of December 12th, 1870. For over a year there had been, as far as was known in the village, no manifestations of any sort at the farm or above it in the sky. It was a moonlit night, cold, frosty and with a rising wind. And at nine o'clock the door of the Lower House opened and Captain John Russell came in, walked over to the counter, asked for a pint of old, and picking up the mug, took a long pull at it and then went over to a settle under the window. There were seven or eight other men in the bar parlor and serving were the proprietor, George Williams, and his wife. Russell spoke to no one and no one addressed him; but such was the effect of this strange coming after so many years of absence that the loud talk in the little room fell away to an almost scared whispering. Russell looked at no one, but stared in front of him; and those who looked at him did so furtively, looking away again quickly. Outside, the noise of the wind increased so that ever and again the door or the windows rattled. And there were other noises outside, or so the men there afterwards declared. Noises up in the air, or so it seemed—whirring noises; "It might have been a train up there," was how one of them described it.

Twice during the hour he was there Captain John Russell walked slowly over to the counter to have his mug refilled. And then at ten o'clock, without a word to anyone, he got up and went out, the wind shrieking as he opened the door and extinguishing one of the lamps.

Captain John Russell

Those left in the bar parlor exchanged glances, but for a while no one spoke. And then George Williams said slowly, "Don't know if it's safe for him to be out by hisself at night."

One of the men in the room said, "You're about right, George!" but no one else spoke.

That was almost the last seen of Captain John Russell. At twelve minutes past ten Coast Guard Herbert Adams, returning to Covehithe along the shore, met him about half a mile from the village and gave him a good night, but received, he said, no reply.

No one ever saw Captain John Russell again, nor was any trace of him ever found; even his footprints along the shore had been washed away by the tide. That was over seventy years ago. Today, the ruin—a shell of four walls—of Spurr Farm still stands and may be seen by the visitor to Covehithe. Something too of the strange events which once happened there are still remembered in the village; but the story as you will hear it from the lips of the grandchildren (themselves now men and women) of those who witnessed them, is a vague and garbled version. The facts are as I have related. As for any explanation which will cover the whole of the phenomena, as well as Russell's life story, I can think of none which is not so fantastic as to be quite incredible.

The Book

by Margaret Irwin

"Then Nora asked, 'What's that red mark on your face?'"

On a foggy night in November, Mr. Corbett, having guessed the murderer by the third chapter of his detective story, arose in disappointment from his bed and went downstairs in search of something more satisfactory to send him to sleep.

The fog had crept through the closed and curtained windows of the dining room and hung thick on the air, in a silence that seemed as heavy and breathless as the fog. The atmosphere was more choking than in his room, and very chill, although the remains of a large fire still burned in the grate.

The dining-room bookcase was the only considerable one in the house, and held a careless, unselected collection to suit all the tastes of the household, together with a few dull and obscure old theological books that had been left over from the sale of a learned uncle's library. Cheap red novels, bought on railway stalls by Mrs. Corbett, who thought a journey the only time to read, were thrust in like pert, undersized intruders among the respectable nineteenth-century works of culture, chastely bound in dark blue or green, which Mr. Corbett had considered the right thing to buy during his Oxford days; beside these there swaggered the children's large, gaily-bound storybooks and collections of fairy tales in every color.

From among this neat, new, clothbound crowd there towered here and there a musty sepulcher of learning, brown with the color of dust rather than leather, with no trace of gilded letters, however faded, on its crumbling back to tell what lay inside. A few of these moribund survivors from the Dean's library were inhospitably fastened with rusty clasps; all remained closed, and appeared impenetrable, their blank forbidding backs uplifted above their frivolous surroundings with the air of scorn that belongs to a private and concealed knowledge. For only the worm of corruption now bored his way through their evil-smelling pages.

It was an unusual flight of fancy for Mr. Corbett to imagine that the vaporous and fog-ridden air that seemed to hang more thickly about the bookcase was like a dank and poisonous breath exhaled by one or other of these slowly rotting volumes. Discomfort in this pervasive and impalpable presence came on him more acutely than at any time that day; in an attempt to clear his throat of it he choked most unpleasantly.

He hurriedly chose a Dickens from the second shelf as appropriate to a London fog, and had returned to the foot of the stairs when he decided that his reading tonight should by contrast be of blue Italian skies and white statues, in beautiful rhythmic sentences. He went back for a Walter Pater.

He found *Marius the Epicurean* tipped sideways across the gap left by his withdrawal of *The Old Curiosity Shop*. It was a very wide gap to have been left by a single volume, for the books on that shelf had been closely wedged together. He put the Dickens back into it and saw that there was still space for a large book. He said to himself in careful and precise words, "This is nonsense. No one can possibly have gone into the dining room and removed a book while I was crossing the hall. There must have been a gap before in the second shelf." But another part of his mind kept saying in a hurried, tumbled torrent, "There was no gap in the second shelf. There was no gap in the second shelf."

He snatched at both the *Marius* and *The Old Curiosity Shop*, and went to his room in a haste that was unnecessary and absurd, since even if he believed in ghosts, which he did not, no one had the smallest reason for suspecting any in the modern Kensington house wherein he and his family had lived for the last fifteen years. Reading was the best thing to calm the nerves, and Dickens a pleasant, wholesome and robust author.

Tonight, however, Dickens struck him in a different light. Beneath the author's sentimental pity for the weak and helpless, he could discern a revolting pleasure in cruelty and suffering, while the grotesque figures of the people in Cruikshank's illustrations revealed too clearly the hideous distortions of their souls. What had seemed humorous now appeared diabolic, and in disgust at these two old favorites, he turned to Walter Pater for the repose and dignity of a classic spirit.

But presently he wondered if this spirit were not in itself of a marble quality, frigid and lifeless, contrary to the purpose of nature. "I have often thought," he said to himself, "that there is something evil in the austere worship of beauty for its own sake." He had never thought so before, but he liked to think that this impulse of fancy was the result of mature consideration, and with this satisfaction he composed himself for sleep.

He woke two or three times in the night, an unusual occurrence, but he was glad of it, for each time he had been dreaming horribly of these blameless Victorian works. Sprightly devils in whiskers and peg-top trousers tortured a lovely maiden and leered in delight at her anguish; the gods and heroes of classic fable acted deeds whose naked crime and shame Mr. Corbett had never appreciated in Latin and Greek Unseens. When he had woken in a cold sweat from the spectacle of the ravished Philomel's torn and bleeding tongue, he decided there was nothing for it but to go down and get another book that would turn his thoughts in some more pleasant direction. But his increasing reluctance to do this found a hundred excuses. The recollection of the gap in the shelf now occurred to him with a sense of unnatural importance; in the troubled dozes that followed, this gap between two books seemed the most hideous deformity, like a gap between the front teeth of some grinning monster.

But in the clear daylight of the morning Mr. Corbett came down to the pleasant dining room, its sunny windows and smell of coffee and toast, and ate an undiminished breakfast with a mind chiefly occupied in self-congratulation that the wind had blown the fog away in time for his Saturday game of golf. Whistling happily, he was pouring out his final cup of coffee, when his hand remained arrested in the act as his glance, roving across to the bookcase, noticed that there was now no gap at all in the second shelf. He asked who had been at the bookcase already, but neither of the girls had, nor Dicky, and Mrs. Corbett was not yet down. The maid never touched the books. They wanted to know what book he missed in it, which made him look foolish, as he could not say. The things that disturb us at midnight are negligible at 9 A.M.

"I thought there was a gap in the second shelf," he said, "but it doesn't matter."

"There never is a gap in the second shelf," said little Jean brightly. "You can take out lots of books from it and when you go back the gap's always filled up. Haven't you noticed that? I have."

Nora, the middle one in age, said Jean was always being silly; she had been found crying over the funny pictures in the *Rose and the Ring* because she said all the people in them had such wicked faces, and the picture of a black cat had upset her because she thought it was a witch. Mr. Corbett did not like to think of such fancies for his Jeannie. She retaliated briskly by saying Dicky was just as bad and he was a big boy. He had kicked a book across the room and said, "Filthy stuff," just like that. Jean was a good mimic; her tone expressed a venom of disgust, and she made the gesture of dropping a book as though the very touch of it were loathsome. Dicky, who had been making violent signs at her, now told her she was a beastly little sneak and he would never again take her for rides on the step of his bicycle. Mr. Corbett was disturbed. Unpleasant housemaids and bad school friends passed through his head, as he gravely asked his son how he had got hold of this book.

"Took it out of that bookcase, of course," said Dicky furiously.

It turned out to be the *Boy's Gulliver's Travels* that Granny had given him, and Dicky had at last to explain his rage with the devil who wrote it to show that men were worse than beasts and the human race a washout. A boy who never had good school reports had no right to be so morbidly sensitive as to penetrate to the underlying cynicism of Swift's delightful fable, and that moreover in the bright and carefully expurgated edition they bring out nowadays. Mr. Corbett could not say he had ever noticed the cynicism himself, though he knew from the critical books it must be there, and with some annoyance he advised his son to take out a nice, bright, modern boy's adventure story that could not depress anybody. It appeared, however, that Dicky was "off reading just now," and the girls echoed this.

Mr. Corbett soon found that he too was "off reading." Every new book seemed to him weak, tasteless and insipid; while his old and familiar books were depressing or even, in some obscure way, disgusting. Authors must all be filthy-minded; they probably wrote what they dared not express in their lives. Stevenson had said that literature was a morbid secretion; he read Stevenson again to discover his peculiar morbidity, and detected in his essays a self-pity masquerading as courage, and in *Treasure Island* an invalid's sickly attraction to brutality.

This gave him a zest to find out what he disliked so much, and his taste for reading revived as he explored with relish the hidden infirmities of minds that had been valued by fools as great and noble. He saw Jane Austen and Charlotte Brontë as two unpleasant examples of spinsterhood; the one as a prying, sub-acid busybody in everyone else's flirtations, the other as a raving, craving mænad seeking self-immolation on the altar of her frustrated passions. He compared Wordsworth's love of nature to the monstrous egoism of an ancient bell-wether, isolated from the flock.

These powers of penetration astonished him. With a mind so acute and original he should have achieved greatness, yet he was a mere solicitor, and not prosperous at that. If he had but the money, he might do something with those ivory shares, but it would be a pure gamble and he had no luck. His natural envy of his wealthier acquaintances now mingled with a contempt for their stupidity that approached loathing. The digestion of his lunch in the City was ruined by meeting sentimental yet successful dotards whom he had once regarded as pleasant fellows. The very sight of them spoiled his game of golf, so that he came to prefer reading alone in the dining room even on sunny afternoons.

He discovered also and with a slight shock that Mrs. Corbett had always bored him. Dicky he began actively to dislike as an impudent blockhead, and the two girls were as insipidly alike as white mice; it was a relief when he abolished their tiresome habit of coming in to say good night.

In the now unbroken silence and seclusion of the dining room, he read with feverish haste as though he were seeking for some clue to knowledge, some secret key to existence which would quicken and inflame it, transform it from its present dull torpor to a life worthy of him and his powers.

He even explored the few decaying remains of his

uncle's theological library. Bored and baffled, he yet persisted, and had the occasional relief of an ugly woodcut of Adam and Eve with figures like bolsters and hair like dahlias, or a map of the Cosmos with Hell-mouth in the corner, belching forth demons. One of these books had diagrams and symbols in the margin which he took to be mathematical formulæ of a kind he did not know. He presently discovered that they were drawn, not printed, and that the book was in manuscript, in a very neat, crabbed black writing that resembled black-letter printing. It was, moreover, in Latin, a fact that gave Mr. Corbett a shock of unreasoning disappointment. For while examining the signs in the margin, he had been filled with an extraordinary exultation, as though he knew himself to be on the edge of a discovery that should alter his whole life. But he had forgotten his Latin.

With a secret and guilty air which would have looked absurd to anyone who knew his harmless purpose, he stole to the schoolroom for Dicky's Latin dictionary and grammar, and hurried back to the dining room, where he tried to discover what the book was about with an anxious industry that surprised himself. There was no name to it, nor of the author. Several blank pages had been left at the end, and the writing ended at the bottom of a page, with no flourish or subscription, as though the book had been left unfinished. From what sentences he could translate, it seemed to be a work on theology rather than mathematics. There were constant references to the Master, to His wishes and injunctions, which appeared to be of a complicated kind. Mr. Corbett began by skipping these as mere accounts of ceremonial, but a word caught his eye as one unlikely to occur in such an account. He read this passage attentively, looking up each word in the dictionary, and could hardly believe the result of his translation. "Clearly," he decided, "this book must be by some early missionary, and the passage I have just read the account of some horrible rite practiced by a savage tribe of devil-worshipers." Though he called it "horrible," he reflected on it, committing each detail to memory. He then amused himself by copying the signs in the margin near it and trying to discover their significance. But a sensation of sickly cold came over him, his head swam, and he could hardly see the figures before his eyes. He suspected a sudden attack of influenza, and went to ask his wife for medicine.

They were all in the drawing room, Mrs. Corbett helping Nora and Jean with a new game, Dicky playing the pianola, and Mike, the Irish terrier, who had lately deserted his accustomed place on the dining-room hearthrug, stretched by the fire. Mr. Corbett had an instant's impression of this peaceful and cheerful scene, before his family turned towards him and asked in scared tones what was the matter. He thought how like sheep they looked and sounded; nothing in his appearance in the mirror struck him as odd; it was their gaping faces that were unfamiliar. He then noticed the extraordinary behavior of Mike, who had sprung from the hearthrug and was crouched in the farthest corner, uttering no sound, but with his eyes distended and foam round his bared teeth. Under Mr. Corbett's glance he slunk towards the door, whimpering in a faint and abject manner, and then, as his master called him, he snarled horribly, and the hair bristled on the scruff of his neck. Dicky let him out, and they heard him scuffling

The Book

at a frantic rate down the stairs to the kitchen, and then, again and again, a long-drawn howl.

"What *can* be the matter with Mike?" asked Mrs. Corbett.

Her question broke a silence that seemed to have lasted a long time. Jean began to cry. Mr. Corbett said irritably that he did not know what was the matter with any of them.

Then Nora asked, "What is that red mark on your face?"

He looked again in the glass and could see nothing.

"It's quite clear from here," said Dicky; "I can see the lines in the fingerprint."

"Yes, that's what it is," said Mrs. Corbett in her brisk, staccato voice; "the print of a finger on your forehead. Have you been writing in red ink?"

Mr. Corbett precipitately left the room for his own, where he sent down a message that he was suffering from headache and would have his dinner in bed. He wanted no one fussing round him. By next morning he was amazed at his fancies of influenza, for he had never felt so well in his life.

No one commented on his looks at breakfast, so he concluded that the mark had disappeared. The old Latin book he had been translating on the previous night had been moved from the writing bureau, although Dicky's grammar and dictionary were still there. The second shelf was, as always in the daytime, closely packed; the book had, he remembered, been in the second shelf. But this time he did not ask who had put it back.

That day he had an unexpected stroke of luck in a new client of the name of Crab, who entrusted him with large sums of money: nor was he irritated by the sight of his more prosperous acquaintances, but with difficulty refrained from grinning in their faces, so confident was he that his remarkable ability must soon place him higher than any of them. At dinner he chaffed his family with what he felt to be the gaiety of a schoolboy. But on them it had a contrary effect, for they stared, either at him in stupid astonishment, or at their plates, depressed and nervous. Did they think him drunk? he wondered, and a fury came on him at their low and bestial suspicions and heavy dullness of mind. Why, he was younger than any of them.

But in spite of this new alertness, he could not attend to the letters he should have written that evening, and drifted to the bookcase for a little light distraction, but found that for the first time there was nothing he wished to read. He pulled out a book from above his head at random, and saw that it was the old Latin book in manuscript. As he turned over its stiff and yellow pages, he noticed with pleasure the smell of corruption that had first repelled him in these decaying volumes, a smell, he now thought, of ancient and secret knowledge.

This idea of secrecy seemed to affect him personally, for on hearing a step in the hall he hastily closed the book and put it back in its place. He went to the schoolroom where Dicky was doing his homework and told him he required his Latin grammar and dictionary again for an old law report. To his annoyance he stammered and put his words awkwardly; he thought that the boy looked oddly at him and he cursed him in his heart for a suspicious young devil, though of what he should be suspicious he could not say. Nevertheless, when back in the dining room, he listened at the door and then softly turned the lock before he opened the books on the writing bureau.

The script and Latin seemed much clearer than on the previous evening, and he was able to read at random a passage relating to the trial of a German midwife in 1620 for the murder and dissection of 783 children. Even allowing for the opportunities afforded by her profession, the number appeared excessive, nor could he discover any motive for the slaughter. He decided to translate the book from the beginning.

It appeared to be an account of some secret society whose activities and ritual were of a nature so obscure, and when not, so vile and terrible, that Mr. Corbett would not at first believe that this could be a record of any human mind, although his deep interest in it should have convinced him that from his humanity, at least, it was not altogether alien.

He read until far later than his usual hour for bed, and when at last he rose, it was with the book in his hands. To defer his parting with it, he stood turning over the pages until he reached the end of the writing, and was struck by a new peculiarity.

The ink was much fresher and of a far poorer quality than the thick, rusted ink in the bulk of the book; on close inspection he would have said that it was of modern manufacture and written quite recently, were it not for the fact that it was in the same crabbed, late-seventeenth-century handwriting.

This, however, did not explain the perplexity, even dismay and fear, he now felt as he stared at the last sentence. It ran, "*Contine te in perennibus studiis,*" and he had at once recognized it as a Ciceronian tag that had been dinned into him at school. He could not understand how he had failed to notice it yesterday.

Then he remembered that the book had ended at the bottom of a page. But now the last two sentences were written at the very top of a page. However long he looked at them, he could come to no other conclusion than that they had been added since the previous evening.

He now read the sentence before the last, "*Re imperfecta mortuus sum*," and translated the whole as, "I died with my purpose unachieved. Continue, thou, the never-ending studies."

With his eyes still fixed upon it, Mr. Corbett replaced the book on the writing bureau and stepped back from it to the door, his hand outstretched behind him, groping and then tugging at the door handle. As the door failed to open, his breath came in a faint, hardly articulate scream. Then he remembered that he had himself locked it, and he fumbled with the key in frantic, ineffectual movements until at last he opened it and banged it after him as he plunged backwards into the hall.

For a moment he stood there looking at the door handle; then with a stealthy, sneaking movement, his hand crept out towards it, touched it, began to turn it, when suddenly he pulled his hand away and went up to his bedroom, three steps at a time.

There he behaved in a manner only comparable with the way he had lost his head after losing his innocence when a schoolboy of sixteen. He hid his face in the pillow, he cried, he raved in meaningless words, repeating, "Never, never, never. I will never do it again. Help me never to do it again." With the words "Help me," he noticed what he was saying, they reminded him of other words, and he began to pray aloud. But the words sounded jumbled; they persisted in coming into his head in a reverse order, so that he found he was saying his prayers backwards, and at this final absurdity he suddenly began to laugh very loud. He sat up on the bed, delighted at this return to sanity, common sense and humor, when the door leading into Mrs. Corbett's room opened, and he saw his wife staring at him with a strange, gray, drawn face that made her seem like the terror-stricken ghost of her usually smug and placid self.

"It's not burglars," he said irritably. "I've come to bed late, that is all, and must have waked you."

"Henry," said Mrs. Corbett, and he noticed that she had not heard him. "Henry, didn't you hear it?"

"What?"

"That laugh."

He was silent, an instinctive caution warning him to wait until she spoke again. And this she did, imploring him with her eyes to reassure her.

"It was not a human laugh. It was like the laugh of a devil."

He checked his violent inclination to laugh again. It was wiser not to let her know that it was only his laughter she had heard. He told her to stop being fanciful, and Mrs. Corbett, gradually recovering her docility, returned to obey an impossible command, since she could not stop being what she had never been.

The next morning, Mr. Corbett rose before any of the servants and crept down to the dining room. As before, the dictionary and grammar alone remained on the writing bureau; the book was back on the second shelf.

He opened it at the end. Two more lines had been added, carrying the writing down to the middle of the page. They ran:

> *Ex auro canceris*
> *In dentem elephantis,*

which he translated as:

> *Out of the money of the crab*
> *Into the tooth of the elephant.*

From this time on, his acquaintances in the City noticed a change in the mediocre, rather flabby and unenterprising "old Corbett." His recent sour depression dropped from him: he seemed to have grown twenty years younger, strong, brisk and cheerful, and with a self-confidence in business that struck them as lunacy. They waited with a not unpleasant excitement for the inevitable crash, but his every speculation, however wild and harebrained, turned out successful. He no longer avoided them, but went out of his way to display his consciousness of luck, daring and vigor, and to chaff them in a manner that began to make him actively disliked. This he welcomed with delight as a sign of others' envy and his superiority.

He never stayed in town for dinners or theaters, for he was always now in a hurry to get home, where, as soon as he was sure of being undisturbed, he would take down the manuscript book from the second shelf of the dining room and turn to the last pages.

Every morning he found that a few words had been added since the evening before, and always they formed, as he considered, injunctions to himself. These were at first only with regard to his money transactions, giving assurance to his boldest fancies, and since the brilliant and unforeseen success that had attended his gamble with Mr. Crab's money in African ivory, he followed all such advice unhesitatingly.

But presently, interspersed with these commands, were others of a meaningless, childish, yet revolting character, such as might be invented by a decadent imbecile, or, it must be admitted, by the idle fancies of any ordinary man who permits his imagination to wander unbridled. Mr. Corbett was startled to recognize one or two such fancies of his own, which had occurred to him during his frequent boredom in church, and which he had not thought any other mind could conceive.

He at first paid no attention to these directions, but found that his new speculations declined so rapidly that he became terrified not merely for his fortune but for his reputation and even safety, since the money of various of his clients was involved. It was made clear to him that he must follow the commands in the book altogether or not at all, and he began to carry out their puerile and grotesque blasphemies with a contemptuous amusement, which, however, gradually changed to a sense of their monstrous significance. They became more capricious and difficult of execution, but he now never hesitated to obey blindly, urged by a fear that he could not understand, but knew only that it was not of mere financial failure.

By now he understood the effect of this book on the others near it, and the reason that had impelled its mysterious agent to move the books into the second shelf so that all in turn should come under the influence of that ancient and secret knowledge.

In respect to it, he encouraged the children, with jeers at their stupidity, to read more, but he could not observe that they ever now took a book from the dining-room bookcase. He himself no longer needed to read, but went to bed early and slept sound. The things that all his life he had longed to do when he should have enough money now seemed to him insipid. His most exciting pleasure was the smell and touch of these moldering pages, as he turned them to find the last message inscribed to him.

One evening it was in two words only, "*Canem occide.*"

He laughed at this simple and pleasant request to kill the dog, for he bore Mike a grudge for his change from devotion to slinking aversion. Moreover, it could not have come more opportunely, since in turning out an old desk he had just discovered some packets of rat poison bought years ago and forgotten. No one therefore knew of its existence, and it would be easy to poison Mike without any further suspicion than that of a neighbor's carelessness. He whistled lightheartedly as he ran upstairs to rummage for the packets, and returned to empty one in the dog's dish of water in the hall.

That night the household was awakened by terrified screams proceeding from the stairs. Mr. Corbett was the first to hasten there, prompted by the instinctive caution that was always with him these days. He saw Jean, in her nightdress, scrambling up on to the landing on her hands and knees, clutching at anything that afforded support and screaming in a choking, tearless, unnatural manner. He carried her to the room she shared with Nora, where they were quickly followed by Mrs. Corbett.

Nothing coherent could be got from Jean. Nora said that she must have been having her old dream again; when her father demanded what this was, she said that Jean sometimes woke in the night, crying, because she had dreamed of a hand passing backwards and forwards over the dining-room bookcase, until it found a certain book and took it out of the shelf. At this point she was always so frightened that she woke up.

On hearing this, Jean broke into fresh screams, and Mrs. Corbett would have no more explanations. Mr. Corbett went out on to the stairs to find what had brought the child there from her bed. On looking down into the lighted hall, he saw Mike's dish overturned. He went down to examine it and saw that the water he had poisoned must have been upset and absorbed by the rough doormat, which was quite wet.

He went back to the little girls' room, told his wife that she was tired and must go to bed, and he would take his turn at comforting Jean. She was now much quieter. He took her on his knee, where at first she shrank from him. Mr. Corbett remembered with an angry sense of injury that she never now sat on his knee, and would have liked to pay her out for it by mocking and frightening her. But he had to coax her into telling him what he wanted, and with this object he soothed her, calling her by pet names that he thought he had forgotten, telling her that nothing could hurt her now he was with her.

At first his cleverness amused him; he chuckled softly when Jean buried her head in his dressing gown.

But presently an uncomfortable sensation came over him, he gripped at Jean as though for her protection, while he was so smoothly assuring her of his. With difficulty he listened to what he had at last induced her to tell him.

She and Nora had kept Mike with them all the evening and taken him to sleep in their room for a treat. He had lain at the foot of Jean's bed and they had all gone to sleep. Then Jean began her old dream of the hand moving over the books in the dining-room bookcase; but instead of taking out a book, it came across the dining room and out on to the stairs. It came up over the banisters and to the door of their room, and turned their door handle very softly and opened it. At this point she jumped up wide awake and turned on the light, calling to Nora. The door, which had been shut when they went to sleep, was wide open, and Mike was gone.

She told Nora that she was sure something dreadful would happen to him if she did not go and bring him back, and ran down into the hall, where she saw him just about to drink from his dish. She called to him and he looked up, but did not come, so she ran to him and began to pull him along with her, when her nightdress was clutched from behind and then she felt a hand seize her arm.

She fell down, and then clambered upstairs as fast as she could, screaming all the way.

It was now clear to Mr. Corbett that Mike's dish must have been upset in the scuffle. She was again crying, but this time he felt himself unable to comfort her. He retired to his room, where he walked up and down in an agitation he could not understand, for he found his thoughts perpetually arguing on a point that had never troubled him before.

"I am not a bad man," he kept saying to himself. "I have never done anything actually wrong. My clients are none the worse for my speculations, only the better. Nor have I spent my new wealth on gross and sensual pleasures; these now have even no attraction for me."

Presently he added: "It is not wrong to try and kill a dog, an ill-tempered brute. It turned against me. It might have bitten Jeannie."

He noticed that he had thought of her as Jeannie, which he had not done for some time; it must have been because he had called her that tonight. He must forbid her ever to leave her room at night, he could not have her meddling. It would be safer for him if she were not there at all.

Again that sick and cold sensation of fear swept over him: he seized the bedpost as though he were falling, and held on to it for some minutes. "I was thinking of a boarding school," he told himself, and then, "I must go down and find out—find out—" He would not think what it was he must find out.

He opened his door and listened. The house was quiet. He crept onto the landing and along to Nora's and Jean's door, where again he stood listening. There was no sound, and at that he was again overcome with unreasonable terror. He imagined Jean lying very still in her bed—too still. He hastened away from the door, shuffling in his bedroom slippers along the passage and down the stairs.

A bright fire still burned in the dining-room grate. A glance at the clock told him it was not yet twelve. He stared at the bookcase. In the second shelf was a gap which had not been there when he had left. On the writing bureau lay a large open book. He knew that he must cross the room and see what was written in it. Then, as before, words that he did not intend came sobbing and crying to his lips, muttering, "No, no, not that. Never, never, never." But he crossed the room and looked down at the book. As last time, the message was in only two words, "*Infantem occide.*"

He slipped and fell forward against the bureau. His hands clutched at the book, lifted it as he recovered himself, and with his finger he traced out the words that had been written. The smell of corruption crept into his nostrils. He told himself that he was not a sniveling dotard, but a man stronger and wiser than his fellows, superior to the common emotions of humanity, who held in his hands the sources of ancient and secret power.

He had known what the message would be. It was after all the only safe and logical thing to do. Jean had acquired dangerous knowledge. She was a spy, an antagonist. That she was so unconsciously, that she was eight years old, his youngest and favorite child, were sentimental appeals that could make no difference to a man of sane reasoning power such as his own. Jean had sided with Mike against him. "All that are not with me are against me," he repeated softly. He would kill both dog and child with the white powder that no one knew to be in his possession. It would be quite safe.

He laid down the book and went to the door. What he had to do he would do quickly, for again that sensation of deadly cold was sweeping over him. He wished he had not to do it tonight; last night would have been

The Book

easier, but tonight she had sat on his knee and made him afraid. He imagined her lying very still in her bed—too still. But it would be she who would lie there, not he, so why should he be afraid? He was protected by ancient and secret powers. He held on to the door handle, but his fingers seemed to have grown numb, for he could not turn it. He clung to it, crouched and shivering, bending over it until he knelt on the ground, his head beneath the handle which he still clutched with upraised hands. Suddenly the hands were loosened and flung outwards with the frantic gesture of a man falling from a great height, and he stumbled to his feet. He seized the book and threw it on the fire. A violent sensation of choking overcame him, he felt he was being strangled, as in a nightmare he tried again and again to shriek aloud, but his breath would make no sound. His breath would not come at all. He fell backwards heavily, down on the floor, where he lay very still.

In the morning the maid who came to open the dining-room windows found her master dead. The sensation caused by this was scarcely so great in the City as that given by the simultaneous collapse of all Mr. Corbett's recent speculations. It was instantly assumed that he must have had previous knowledge of this and so committed suicide.

The stumbling block of this theory was that the medical report defined the cause of Mr. Corbett's death as strangulation of the windpipe by the pressure of a hand which had left the marks of its fingers on his throat.

Dracula's Guest

by Bram Stoker

When one is alone, one shouldn't wander too far afield on Walpurgis Night.

When we started for our drive the sun was shining brightly on Munich, and the air was full of the joyousness of early summer. Just as we were about to depart, Herr Delbrück (the maître d'hôtel of the Quatre Saisons, where I was staying) came down, bareheaded, to the carriage and, after wishing me a pleasant drive, said to the coachman, still holding his hand on the handle of the carriage door,

"Remember you are back by nightfall. The sky looks bright, but there is a shiver in the north wind that says there may be a sudden storm. But I am sure you will not be late." Here he smiled, and added, "For you know what night it is."

Johann answered with an emphatic, "Ja, mein Herr," and, touching his hat, drove off quickly. When we had cleared the town, I said, after signaling to him to stop, "Tell me, Johann, what is tonight?"

He crossed himself, as he answered laconically, "Walpurgisnacht." Then he took out his watch, a great, old-fashioned German-silver thing as big as a turnip, and looked at it, with his eyebrows gathered together and a little impatient shrug of his shoulders. I realized that this was his way of respectfully protesting against the unnecessary delay, and sank back in the carriage, merely motioning him to proceed. He started off rapidly, as if to make up for lost time. Every now and then the horses seemed to throw up their heads and sniff the air suspiciously. On such occasions I often looked round in alarm. That road was pretty bleak, for we were traversing a sort of high, windswept plateau. As we drove, I saw a road that looked but little used, and which seemed to dip through a little winding valley. It looked so inviting that, even at the risk of offending him, I called Johann to stop. And when he had pulled up I told him I would like to drive down that road. He made all sorts of excuses, and frequently crossed himself as he spoke. This somewhat piqued my curiosity, so I asked him various questions. He answered fencingly, and repeatedly looked at his watch in protest. Finally I said,

"Well, Johann, I want to go down this road. I shall not ask you to come unless you like; but tell me why you do not like to go, that is all I ask." For answer he seemed to throw himself off the box, so quickly did he reach the ground. Then he stretched out his hands appealing to me, and implored me not to go. There was just enough of English mixed with the German for me to understand the drift of his talk. He seemed always just about to tell me something—the very idea of which evidently frightened him; but each time he pulled himself up, saying, as he crossed himself, "Walpurgisnacht!"

I tried to argue with him, but it was difficult to argue with a man when I did not know his language. The advantage certainly rested with him, for although he began to speak in English—of a very crude and broken kind—he always got excited and broke into his native tongue—and every time he did so he looked at his watch. Then the horses became restless and sniffed the air. At this he grew very pale, and, looking around in a frightened way, he suddenly jumped forward, took them by the bridles and led them on some twenty feet. I followed, and asked why he had done this. For answer he crossed himself, pointed to the spot we had left, and drew his carriage in the direction of the other road, indicating a cross, and said, first in German, then in English, "Buried him—him what killed themselves."

I remembered the old custom of burying suicides at crossroads. "Ah! I see, a suicide. How interesting!" But for the life of me I could not make out why the horses were frightened.

Whilst we were talking, we heard a sort of sound between a yelp and a bark. It was far away; but the horses got very restless, and it took Johann all his time to quiet them. He was pale, and said: "It sounds like a wolf—but yet there are no wolves here now."

"No?" I said, questioning him; "isn't it long since the wolves were so near the city?"

"Long, long," he answered, "in the spring and summer; but with the snow the wolves have been here not so long."

Whilst he was petting the horses and trying to quiet

them, dark clouds drifted rapidly across the sky. The sunshine passed away, and a breath of cold wind seemed to drift past us. It was only a breath, however, and more in the nature of a warning than a fact, for the sun came out brightly again. Johann looked under his lifted hand at the horizon and said,

"The storm of snow, he comes before long time." Then he looked at his watch again, and, straightway, holding his reins firmly—for the horses were still pawing the ground restlessly, and shaking their heads—he climbed to his box as though the time had come for proceeding on our journey.

I felt a little obstinate, and did not at once get into the carriage.

"Tell me," I said, "about this place where the road leads." And I pointed down.

Again he crossed himself and mumbled a prayer, before he answered, "It is unholy."

"What is unholy?" I enquired.

"The village."

"Then there is a village?"

"No, no. No one lives there hundreds of years."

My curiosity was piqued. "But you said there was a village."

"There was."

"Where is it now?"

Whereupon he burst out into a long story in German and English, so mixed up that I could not quite understand exactly what he said, but roughly I gathered that long ago, hundreds of years, men had died there and been buried in their graves; and sounds were heard under the clay, and when the graves were opened, men and women were found rosy with life, and their mouths red with blood. And so, in haste to save their lives (aye, and their souls!—and here he crossed himself), those who were left fled away to other places, where the living lived, and the dead were dead and not—not something. He was evidently afraid to speak the last words. As he proceeded with his narration, he grew more and more excited. It seemed as if his imagination had got hold of him, and he ended in a perfect paroxysm of fear—white-faced, perspiring, trembling and looking round him, as if expecting that some dreadful presence would manifest itself there in the bright sunshine on the open plain. Finally, in an agony of desperation, he cried,

"Walpurgisnacht!" and pointed to the carriage for me to get in. All my English blood rose at this, and, standing back, I said:

"You are afraid, Johann—you are afraid. Go home; I shall return alone; the walk will do me good." The carriage door was open. I took from the seat my oak walking stick—which I always carry on my holiday excursions—and closed the door, pointing back to Munich, and said, "Go home, Johann—Walpurgisnacht doesn't concern Englishmen."

The horses were now more restive than ever, and Johann was trying to hold them in, while excitedly imploring me not to do anything so foolish. I pitied the poor fellow, he was so deeply in earnest; but all the same I could not help laughing. His English was quite gone now. In his anxiety he had forgotten that his only means of making me understand was to talk my language, so he jabbered away in his native German. It began to be a little tedious. After giving the direction,

"Home!" I turned to go down the crossroad into the valley.

With a despairing gesture, Johann turned his horses towards Munich. I leaned on my stick and looked after him. He went slowly along the road for a while; then there came over the crest of the hill a man tall and thin. I could see so much in the distance. When he drew near the horses, they began to jump and kick about, then to scream with terror. Johann could not hold them in; they bolted down the road, running away madly. I watched them out of sight, then looked for the stranger, but I found that he, too, was gone.

With a light heart I turned down the side road through the deepening valley to which Johann had objected. There was not the slightest reason, that I could see, for his objection; and I dare say I tramped for a couple of hours without thinking of time or distance, and certainly without seeing a person or a house. So far as the place was concerned, it was desolation itself. But I did not notice this particularly till, on turning a bend in the road, I came upon a scattered fringe of wood; then I recognized that I had been impressed unconsciously by the desolation of the region through which I had passed.

I sat down to rest myself, and began to look around. It struck me that it was considerably colder than it had been at the commencement of my walk—a sort of sighing sound seemed to be around me, with, now and then, high overhead, a sort of muffled roar. Looking upwards, I noticed that great thick clouds were drifting rapidly across the sky from north to south at a great height. There were signs of coming storm in some lofty stratum of the air. I was a little chilly, and, thinking that it was the sitting still after the exercise of walking, I resumed my journey.

The ground I passed over was now much more picturesque. There were no striking objects that the eye might single out; but in all there was a charm of beauty. I took little heed of time and it was only when the deepening twilight forced itself upon me that I began to think of how I should find my way home. The brightness of the day had gone. The air was cold, and the drifting of clouds high overhead was more marked. They were accompanied by a sort of faraway rushing sound, through which seemed to come at intervals that mysterious cry which the driver had said came from a wolf. For a while I hesitated. I had said I would see the deserted village, so on I went, and presently came on a wide stretch of open country shut in by hills all around. Their sides were covered with trees, which spread down to the plain, dotting, in clumps, the gentler slopes and hollows which showed here and there. I followed with my eye the winding of the road, and saw that it curved close to one of the densest of these clumps and was lost behind it.

As I looked there came a cold shiver in the air, and the snow began to fall. I thought of the miles and miles of bleak country I had passed, and then hurried on to seek the shelter of the wood in front. Darker and darker grew the sky, and faster and heavier fell the snow, till the earth before and around me was a glistening white carpet the farther edge of which was lost in misty vagueness. The road was here but crude, and, when on the level, its boundaries were not so marked as when it passed through the cuttings; and in a little while I found that I must have strayed from it, for I missed underfoot the hard surface, and my feet sank deeper in the grass and moss. Then the wind grew stronger and blew with ever-increasing force, till I was fain to run before it. The air became icy cold, and in spite of my exercise I began to suffer. The snow was now falling so thickly and whirling around me in such rapid eddies that I could hardly keep my eyes open. Every now and then the heavens were torn asunder by vivid lightning, and in the flashes I could see ahead of me a great mass of trees, chiefly yew and cypress, all heavily coated with snow.

I was soon amongst the shelter of the trees, and there, in comparative silence, I could hear the rush of the wind high overhead. Presently the blackness of the storm had become merged in the darkness of the night. By and by the storm seemed to be passing away; it now only came in fierce puffs or blasts. At such moments the weird sound of the wolf appeared to be echoed by many similar sounds around me.

Now and again, through the black mass of drifting cloud, came a straggling ray of moonlight, which lit up the expanse, and showed me that I was at the edge of a dense mass of cypress and yew trees. As the snow had ceased to fall, I walked out from the shelter and began to investigate more closely. It appeared to me that, amongst so many old foundations as I had passed, there might be still standing a house in which, though in ruins, I could find some sort of shelter for a while. As I skirted the edge of the copse, I found that a low wall encircled it, and following this I presently found an opening. Here the cypresses formed an alley leading up to a square mass of some kind of building. Just as I caught sight of this, however, the drifting clouds obscured the moon, and I passed up the path in darkness. The wind must have grown colder, for I felt myself shiver as I walked; but there was hope of shelter, and I groped my way blindly on.

I stopped, for there was a sudden stillness. The storm had passed; and, perhaps in sympathy with Nature's silence, my heart seemed to cease to beat. But this was only momentarily; for suddenly the moonlight broke through the clouds, showing me that I was in a graveyard, and that the square object before me was a great massive tomb of marble, as white as the snow that lay on and all around it. With the moonlight there came a fierce sigh of the storm, which appeared to resume its course with a long, low howl, as of many dogs or wolves. I was awed and shocked, and felt the cold perceptibly grow upon me till it seemed to grip me by the heart. Then, while the flood of moonlight still fell on the marble tomb, the storm gave further evidence of renewing—as though it was returning on its track. Impelled by some sort of fascination, I approached the sepulcher to see what it was, and why such a thing stood alone in such a place. I walked around it, and read, over the Doric door, in German:

COUNTESS DOLINGER OF GRATZ
IN STYRIA
SOUGHT AND FOUND DEAD
1801

On the top of the tomb, seemingly driven through the solid marble—for the structure was composed of a few vast blocks of stone—was a great iron spike or stake. On going to the back I saw, graven in great Russian letters:

The dead travel fast.

There was something so weird and uncanny about the whole thing that it gave me a turn and made me feel quite faint. I began to wish, for the first time, that I had taken Johann's advice. Here a thought struck me, which came under almost mysterious circumstances and with a terrible shock. This was Walpurgis Night!

Walpurgis Night, when, according to the belief of millions of people, the devil was abroad—when the graves were opened and the dead came forth and walked. When all evil things of earth and air and water held revel. This very place the driver had specially shunned. This was the depopulated village of centuries ago. This was where the suicide lay; and this was the place where I was alone—unmanned, shivering with cold in a shroud of snow with a wild storm gathering again upon me! It took all my philosophy, all the religion I had been taught, all my courage, not to collapse in a paroxysm of fright.

And now a perfect tornado burst upon me. The ground shook as though thousands of horses thundered across it; and this time the storm bore on its icy wings, not snow, but great hailstones which drove with such violence that they might have come from the thongs of Balearic slingers—hailstones that beat down leaf and branch and made the shelter of the cypresses of no more avail than though their stems were standing corn. At the first I had rushed to the nearest tree; but I was soon fain to leave it and seek the only spot that seemed to afford refuge, the deep Doric doorway of the marble tomb. There, crouching against the massive bronze door, I gained a certain amount of protection from the beating of the hailstones, for now they only drove against me as they richocheted from the ground and the side of the marble.

As I leaned against the door it moved slightly and opened inwards. The shelter of even a tomb was welcome in that pitiless tempest, and I was about to enter it when there came a flash of forked lightning that lit up the whole expanse of the heavens. In the instant, as I am a living man, I saw, as my eyes were turned into the darkness of the tomb, a beautiful woman, with rounded cheeks and red lips, seemingly sleeping on a bier. As the thunder broke overhead, I was grasped as by the hand of a giant and hurled out into the storm. The whole thing was so sudden that, before I could realize the shock, moral as well as physical, I found the hailstones beating me down. At the same time I had a strange, dominating feeling that I was not alone. I looked towards the tomb. Just then there came another blinding flash, which seemed to strike the iron stake that surmounted the tomb and to pour through to the earth, blasting and crumbling the marble, as in a burst of flame. The dead woman rose for a moment of agony, while she was lapped in the flame, and her bitter scream of pain was drowned in the thundercrash. The last thing I heard was this mingling of dreadful sound, as again I was seized in the giant grasp and dragged away, while the hailstones beat on me, and the air around seemed reverberant with the howling of wolves. The last sight that I remembered was a vague, white, moving mass, as if all the graves around me had sent out the phantoms of their sheeted dead, and they were closing in on me through the white cloudiness of the driving hail.

Gradually there came a sort of vague beginning of consciousness; then a sense of weariness that was dreadful. For a time I remembered nothing; but slowly my senses returned. My feet seemed positively racked with pain, yet I could not move them. They seemed to be numbed. There was an icy feeling at the back of my neck and all down my spine, and my ears, like my feet, were dead, yet in torment, but there was in my breast a sense of warmth which was, by comparison, delicious. It was as a nightmare—a physical nightmare, if one may use such an expression; for some heavy weight on my chest made it difficult for me to breathe.

This period of semi-lethargy seemed to remain a long time, and as it faded away I must have slept or swooned. Then came a sort of loathing, like the first stage of seasickness, and a wild desire to be free from something—I knew not what. A vast stillness enveloped me, as though all the world were asleep or dead—only broken by the low panting as of some animal close to me. I felt a warm rasping at my throat, then came a consciousness of the awful truth, which chilled me to the heart and sent the blood surging up through my brain. Some great animal was lying on me and now licking my throat. I feared to stir, for some instinct of prudence made me lie still; but the brute seemed to realize that there was now some change in me, for it raised its head. Through my eyelashes I saw above me the two great flaming eyes of a gigantic wolf. Its sharp white teeth gleamed in the gaping red mouth, and I could feel its hot breath fierce and acrid upon me.

For another spell of time I remembered no more. Then I became conscious of a low growl, followed by a yelp, renewed again and again. Then, seemingly very far away, I heard a "Holloa! Holloa!" as of many voices calling in unison. Cautiously I raised my head and looked in the direction whence the sound came; but the cemetery blocked my view. The wolf still continued to yelp in a strange way, and a red glare began to move round the grove of cypresses, as though following the sound. As the voices drew closer, the wolf yelped faster and louder. I feared to make either sound or motion. Nearer came the red glow, over the white pall which stretched into the darkness around me. Then all at once from beyond the trees there came at a trot a troop of horsemen bearing torches. The wolf rose from my breast and made for the cemetery. I saw one of the horsemen (soldiers by their caps and their long military cloaks) raise his carbine and take aim. A companion knocked up his arm, and I heard the ball whiz over my head. He had evidently taken my body for that of the wolf. Another sighted the animal as it slunk away, and a shot followed. Then, at a gallop, the troop rode forward; some towards me, others following the wolf as it disappeared amongst the snow-clad cypresses.

As they drew nearer I tried to move, but was powerless, although I could see and hear all that went on around me. Two or three of the soldiers jumped from their horses and knelt beside me. One of them raised my head, and placed his hand over my heart.

"Good news, comrades!" he cried. "His heart still beats!"

Then some brandy was poured down my throat; it

put vigor into me, and I was able to open my eyes fully and look around. Lights and shadows were moving among the trees, and I heard men call to one another. They drew together uttering frightened exclamations; and the lights flashed as the others came pouring out of the cemetery pell-mell, like men possessed. When the farther ones came close to us, those who were around me asked them eagerly,

"Well, have you found him?"

The reply rang out hurriedly,

"No! No! Come away quick—quick! This is no place to stay, and on this of all nights!"

"What was it?" was the question, asked in all manner of keys. The answer came variously and all indefinitely as though the men were moved by some common impulse to speak, yet were restrained by some common fear from giving their thoughts.

"It—it—indeed!" gibbered one, whose wits had plainly given out for the moment.

"A wolf—and yet not a wolf!" another put in shudderingly.

"No use trying for him without the sacred bullet," a third remarked in a more ordinary manner.

"Serve us right for coming out on this night! Truly we have earned our thousand marks!" were the ejaculations of a fourth.

"There was blood on the broken marble," another said after a pause; "the lightning never brought that there. And for him—is he safe? Look at his throat! See, comrades, the wolf has been lying on him and keeping his blood warm."

The officer looked at my throat and replied,

"He is all right; the skin is not pierced. What does it all mean? We should never have found him but for the yelping of the wolf."

"What became of it?" asked the man who was holding up my head, and who seemed the least panic-stricken of the party, for his hands were steady and without tremor. On his sleeve was the chevron of a petty officer.

"It went to its home," answered the man, whose long face was pallid, and who actually shook with terror as he glanced around him fearfully. "There are graves enough there in which it may lie. Come, comrades— come quickly! Let us leave this cursed spot."

The officer raised me to a sitting posture as he uttered a word of command; then several men placed me upon a horse. He sprang to the saddle behind me, took me in his arms, gave the word to advance; and, turning our faces away from the cyprooooo, we rode away in swift, military order.

As yet my tongue refused its office, and I was perforce silent. I must have fallen asleep; for the next thing I remembered was finding myself standing up, supported by a soldier on each side of me. It was almost broad daylight, and to the north a red streak of sunlight was reflected, like a path of blood, over the waste of snow. The officer was telling the men to say nothing of what they had seen, except that they found an English stranger, guarded by a large dog.

"Dog! That was no dog," cut in the man who had exhibited such fear. "I think I know a wolf when I see one."

The young officer answered calmly, "I said a dog."

"Dog!" reiterated the other ironically. It was evident that his courage was rising with the sun; and, pointing to me, he said, "Look at his throat. Is that the work of a dog, master?"

Instinctively I raised my hand to my throat, and as I touched it I cried out in pain. The men crowded round to look, some stooping down from their saddles; and again there came the calm voice of the young officer, "A dog, as I said. If aught else were said we should only be laughed at."

I was then mounted behind a trooper, and we rode on into the suburbs of Munich. Here we came across a stray carriage, into which I was lifted, and it was driven off to the Quatre Saisons—the young officer accompanying me, whilst a trooper followed with his horse, and the others rode off to their barracks.

When we arrived, Herr Delbrück rushed so quickly down the steps to meet me that it was apparent he had been watching within. Taking me by both hands he solicitously led me in. The officer saluted me and was turning to withdraw, when I recognized his purpose, and insisted that he should come to my rooms. Over a glass of wine I warmly thanked him and his brave comrades for saving me. He replied simply that he was more than glad, and that Herr Delbrück had at the first taken steps to make all the searching party pleased; at which ambiguous utterance the maître d'hôtel smiled, while the officer pleaded duty and withdrew.

"But Herr Delbrück," I inquired, "how and why was it that the soldiers searched for me?"

He shrugged his shoulders, as if in depreciation of his own deed, as he replied,

"I was so fortunate as to obtain leave, from the commander of the regiment in which I served, to ask for volunteers."

"But how did you know I was lost?" I asked.

"The driver came hither with the remains of his carriage, which had been upset when the horses ran away."

"But surely you would not send a search party of soldiers merely on this account?"

"Oh no!" he answered; "but even before the coachman arrived, I had this telegram from the Boyar whose guest you are," and he took from his pocket a telegram, which he handed to me, and I read,

Bistrize.

Be careful of my guest—his safety is most precious to me. Should aught happen to him, or if he be missed, spare nothing to find him and ensure his safety. He is English and therefore adventurous. There are often dangers from snow and wolves and night. Lose not a moment if you suspect harm to him. I answer your zeal with my fortune.

Dracula.

As I held the telegram in my hand, the room seemed to whirl around me; and, if the attentive maître d'hôtel had not caught me, I think I should have fallen. There was something so strange in all this, something so weird and impossible to imagine, that there grew on me a sense of my being in some way the sport of opposite forces—the mere vague idea of which seemed in a way to paralyze me. I was certainly under some form of mysterious protection. From a distant country had come, in the very nick of time, a message that took me out of the danger of the snow-sleep and the jaws of the wolf.

The Cocoon

by John B. L. Goodwin

"Denny shuddered and closed his eyes."

Whereas downstairs his father had a room the walls of which were studded with the trophies of his aggressive quests: heads of ibex, chamois, eland, keitloa, peccary, and ounce, upstairs Denny had pinned upon his playroom walls the fragile bodies of Swallowtails, Nymphs, Fritillaries, Meadow Browns, and Anglewings.

Although his father had maneuvered expeditions, experienced privation, waded through jungles, climbed upon crags for his specimens, Denny had blithely gathered his within the fields and gardens close to home. It was likely that his father's day as a collector was over; Denny's had just begun.

Denny was eleven and his father forty-six and the house in which they lived was a hundred or more years old though no one could be exact about it. Mr. Peatybog, the postmaster in the shriveled village, said as how he could recall when the circular window on the second-story landing hadn't been there and Mrs. Bliss said she knew that at one time what was now the kitchen had been a taproom because her father had told her about it. The heart of the house, as Denny's father put it, was very old but people had altered it and added on and covered up. Denny's father had added the room where his heads were hung, but Denny's playroom must have been the original attic because where the rafters of its high, abrupt ceiling were visible the nails in them were square-headed and here and there the timbers were still held together with wooden pegs.

But the playroom, where Denny also slept, appeared to the casual glance anything but old. The floor was carpeted in blue, the curtains were yellow and the bedspread blue and white. The wallpaper, which his mother had chosen for him before she left, was yellow willow trees on a pale blue ground and to an alien eye the butterflies pinned on the walls seemed part of the design. It had been a long time since Denny's father had been up in the room and although he knew that his son's collection of Lepidoptera, as he called them, was pinned upon the walls he did not know and therefore could not reprimand his son for the damage they had done the pretty wallpaper. Under each specimen a putty-colored blot was spreading over the blue paper. It was the oil exuding from the drying bodies of the dead insects.

In one corner of the room was a chintz-covered chest in which lay the remains of Denny's earlier loves; battered trains and sections of track, an old transformer, batteries covered with cavern-like crystals of zinc salts, trucks, and windmills no longer recognizable as much more than haphazard, wooden arrangements of fitted blocks and sticks, books crumpled and torn with Denny's name or current dream scrawled aggressively

The Cocoon

in crayon across the print and pictures, a gyroscope, a rubber ball, its cracked paint making a mosaic of antique red and gold around its sphere, and somewhere at the bottom, weighed down with tin and lead and wood more than any corpse with earth and grass, lay a bear, a monkey, and a boy doll with a scar across one cheek where Denny had kicked it with a skate. In another corner the symbols of his present were proudly displayed. The butterfly net leaned against the wall, and close to the floor on a wooden box turned upside down stood Denny's cyanide bottle, tweezers, and pins, the last shining as dangerously bright as minute surgical instruments in their packet of black paper.

After almost a year of collecting butterflies, Denny had found that a certain equivocal quality could be added to his pursuit if he were to collect not only the butterflies but also the earlier stages of their mutations. By cramming milk bottles, shoe boxes, and whatever other receptacle the house might offer with caterpillars and pupae he was, in the cases of those that survived, able to participate in a sort of alchemy. Intently he would squat on his haunches and gaze into the receptacles, studying the laborious transformations, the caterpillar shedding skin, the exudation that it used to hitch its shroudlike chrysalid to twigs or undersides of leaves, and then the final unpredictable attainment of the imago. It was like opening a surprise package. For as yet Denny had not learned to tell what color, size, or shape worm would turn into a Dog's Head Sulphur, Mourning Cloak, or Tiger Swallowtail.

As late summer approached, Denny insisted that the servant girl refrain from opening the windows wide in order to air out his room. The sudden change in temperature, he said, would disturb the caterpillars and pupae. Even though the girl reported to his father that Denny's room smelled unheathily from all the bugs and things, the man did no more than mention it to Denny in an offhand manner. Denny grunted to show that he had heard and did no more about it, and as his father was writing a book on his jungles and crags and beasts, he had really very little concern about what went on upstairs.

So it was that an arid smell of decaying vegetable matter resolving itself into insect flesh pervaded Denny's bright attic room and the oily blotches on the walls beneath his specimens spread ever so slightly, discoloring the paper more and more.

In a book, *Butterflies You Ought to Know Better*, which an aunt had sent him for Christmas, Denny read that a suitable "castle" for a caterpillar could be made by placing a lamp chimney, closed at the top, upon a flowerpot filled with earth. He prepared this enclosure, purchasing the lamp chimney from the village store with his own money. It was such an elegant contrivance and yet so magical that he decided to save it for an especially unusual specimen. It was not until a late afternoon in October that Denny found one worthy of the "castle."

He was exploring a copse between two fields. Because of the stoniness of its ground it had never been cultivated and lay like a sword between the fertility of the fields on either side. Denny had never trespassed on it before and dared to now only because of his growing self-confidence in his power over nature. A month ago he would have shied away from the area entirely, even taking the precaution to circumvent the two fields enclosing it. But he felt a little now the way he thought God must feel when, abject within its glass and cardboard world, the life he watched took form, changed, and ceased. Protected from unpleasant touch of any unpredictable action, Denny watched the metamorphosis from worm to chrysalid to miraculously vibrant petal. It lay within his power to sever abruptly the magical chain of their evolution at any point he chose. In a little way he was a little like God. It was this conceit that now gave him the courage to climb over the stones of the old wall and enter the half acre of dense woodland.

The autumn sun, already low, ogled the brittle landscape like some improbable jack-o'-lantern hanging in the west. What birds were still in that country spoke in the rasping tone of the herd; the more mellifluous and prosperous had already gone south. Although the leaves on the trees displayed the incautious yellows of senility and ochres of decay, the underbrush such as catbrier and wild grape were mostly green. Armed with his forceps and his omnipotence, Denny explored each living leaf and twig.

Brambles tore his stockings and scratched his knees but, except for vulgar tent caterpillars in the wild cherry trees, Denny's efforts went unrewarded. It was dusk when, searching among the speculatively shaped leaves of a sassafras, Denny found a specimen beyond his most arrogant expectations. At first sight, due in part to the twilight, it looked more like some shriveled dragon than a caterpillar. Between it and the twig a filament stretched and this, added to the fact that when Denny touched it gingerly he could feel its puffy flesh contract the way caterpillars do, convinced him that it was no freak of nature or if it was it was a caterpillar freak and therefore nothing to fear. Tearing it cautiously with his tweezers from the twig, he put the monster in the Diamond Match box he always carried with him and, running breathlessly, blind to brier and brambles, Denny headed home.

It was suppertime when he got there and his father was already at the table, his left hand turning the pages of a book while with his right hand he ladled soup into his mouth. Denny had clattered up the stairs before his father was aware of his presence.

"You're late, son," he said in the moment between two printed sentences and two spoonfuls of soup.

"I know, Father," Denny replied without stopping, "but I got something."

Another sentence and another spoonful.

"How many times have I told you to be explicit? *Something* can be anything from a captive balloon to a case of mumps."

From the second landing Denny called down, "It's just *something*. I don't know exactly what it is."

His father mumbled, and by the time he had finished a paragraph and scooped up the last nugget of meat out of his soup and had addressed his son with the words, "Whatever it is it will wait until you have your supper," Denny was peering at it through the glass of the lamp chimney.

Even in the bright electric glare it was reptilian. It was large for a caterpillar, between four and five inches long Denny guessed, and was a muddy purple color, its underside a yellowish black. At either extremity it bore a series of three horny protuberances of a vermilion shade; they were curved sharply inward and stiff little hairs grew from them. From its mouth there protruded a set of small grasping claws like those of a crustacean. Its skin was wrinkled like that of a tortoise and the abdominal segments were sharply defined. The feet lacked the usual suctionlike apparatuses caterpillars have but were scaly and shaped like tiny claws.

It was indeed worthy of its "castle." It was not to be found in any of the illustrated books Denny had. He would guard it and keep it a secret and finally, when he presented its metamorphosis into a winged thing to the world, his father's renown as the captor of extraordinary beasts would pale beside his own. The only thing he could guess at, and that because of its size, was that it was the larva of a moth rather than that of a butterfly.

He was still peering at it when the servant girl brought up a tray. "Here," she said, "if you're such a busy little gentleman that you can't spare time for supper like an ordinary boy. If I had my way you'd go hungry." She set the tray down on a table. "Pugh!" she added. "The smell in this room is something awful. What have you got there now?" And she was about to peer over Denny's shoulder.

"Get out!" he shrieked, turning on her. "Get out!"

"I'm not so sure I will if you speak like that."

He arose and in his fury pushed her hulk out the door, slamming it and locking it after her.

She started to say something on the other side, but what it was Denny never knew or cared, for his own voice screaming, "And stay out!" sent the young girl scurrying down the stairs to his father.

It was typical of the man that he merely commiserated with the girl, agreed with her on the urgency of some sort of discipline for his son, and then, settling back to his pipe and his manuscript, dismissed the matter from his mind.

The following day Denny told the girl that henceforth she was not to enter his room, neither to make the bed nor to clean.

"We shall see about that," she said, "though it would be a pleasure such as I never hoped for this side of heaven were I never to enter that horrid smelling room again."

Again his father was approached and this time he reluctantly called his son to him.

"Ethel tells me something about you not wanting her to go into your room," he said, peering over his glasses.

"I'd rather she didn't, Father," Denny replied, humble as pie. "You see, she doesn't understand about caterpillars and cocoons and things and she messes everything up."

"But who will see to the making of your bed and dusting and such?"

"I will," asserted Denny. "There's no reason why if I don't want anyone to go into my room I shouldn't have to make up for it somehow, like making my own bed and clearing up."

"Spoken like a soldier, son," the father said. "I know the way you feel and if you're willing to pay the price in responsibility I see no reason why you shouldn't have your wish. But," and he pointed a paper-knife of walrus tusk at the boy, "if it isn't kept neat and tidy we'll have to rescind the privilege; remember that."

His father, grateful that the interview had not been as tedious as he had anticipated, told his son he could

The Cocoon

go. From then on Denny always kept the key to his room in his pocket.

Because caterpillars cease to eat prior to their chrysalis stage and Denny's caterpillar refused to eat whatever assortment of leaves he tried to tempt it with, Denny knew that it had definitely been preparing its cocoon when he had plucked it from the sassafras branch. It was very restless, almost convulsive now, and within the lamp chimney it humped itself aimlessly from twig to twig, its scaly little claws searching for something to settle upon. After a day of such meanderings the caterpillar settled upon a particular crotch of the twig and commenced to spin its cocoon. By the end of twenty-four hours the silken alembic was complete.

Though there was now nothing for Denny to observe, he still squatted for hours on end staring at the cocoon that hung like some parasitic growth from the sassafras twig. His concentration upon the shape was so great as he sat hunched over it, that his eyes seemed to tear the silken shroud apart and to be intimately exploring the secret that was taking place within.

Now Denny spent less and less of the days out in the open searching for the more common types of chrysalid with which he was acquainted. Such were for him as garnets would be to a connoisseur of emeralds. His lean, tanned face became puffy and the palms of his hands were pale and moist.

The winter months dragged on and Denny was as listlessly impatient as what was inside the cocoon. His room was cold and airless, for a constant low temperature must be kept if the cocoon was to lie dormant until spring. His bed was seldom made and the floor was thick with dust and mud. Once a week the girl left the broom and dustpan along with the clean sheets outside his door, but Denny took only the sheets into his room where they would collect into a stack on the floor for weeks at a time. His father took no notice of his condition other than to write in a postscript to what was otherwise a legal and splenetic letter to his wife that their son looked peaked and upon receiving an apprehensive reply he casually asked Denny if he was feeling all right. The boy's affirmative though noncommittal answer seemed to satisfy him and, dropping a card to his wife to the effect that their son professed to be in sound health, he considered himself released from any further responsibility.

When April was about gone Denny moved his treasure close to the window where the sun would induce the dormant thing within it into life. In a few days Denny was sure that it was struggling for release, for the cocoon seemed to dance up and down idiotically upon its thread. All that night he kept vigil, his red and swollen eyes focused on the cocoon as upon some hypnotic object. His father ate breakfast alone and by nine o'clock showed enough concern to send the servant girl up to see if everything was all right. She hurried back to report that his son was at least still alive enough to be rude to her. The father mumbled something in reply about the boy's mother having shirked her responsibilities. The girl said that if it pleased him, she would like to give notice. She was very willing to enumerate the reasons why, but the man dismissed her casually with the request that she stay until she found someone to take her place.

The Cocoon

At ten Denny was positive that the cocoon was about to break; by ten-thirty there was no longer any doubt in his mind. Somewhat before eleven the eclosion took place. There was a convulsive movement inside and the cocoon opened at the top with the faint rustle of silk. The feathery antennae and the two forelegs issued forth, the legs clutching the cocoon in order to hoist the body through the narrow aperture. The furry and distended abdomen, upon which were hinged the crumpled wings, was drawn out with effort. Immediately the creature commenced awkwardly to climb the twig from which the cocoon was suspended. Denny watched the procedure in a trance. Having gained the tip of the branch and unable to proceed farther, the insect rested, its wings hanging moist and heavy from its bloated body. The abdomen with each pulsation shrank visibly and gradually, very gradually, the antennae unfurled and the wings expanded with the juices pumped into them from the body.

Within an hour the metamorphosis of many months was complete. The beast, its wings still slightly damp though fully spread, fluttered gently before the eyes of the boy. Though escaped from its cocoon, it lay imprisoned still behind the glass.

Denny's pallor was suddenly flushed. He grasped the lamp chimney as if he would hold the insect to him. This was his miracle, his alone. He watched with a possessive awe as the creature flexed its wings, although it was still too weak to attempt flight. Surely this specimen before him was unique. The wings were easily ten inches across and their color was so subtly gradated that it was impossible to say where black turned to purple and purple to green and green back into black.

The only definite delineations were a crablike simulacrum centered on each hind wing and upon each fore wing, the imitation of an open mouth with teeth bared. Both the crabs and the mouths were chalked in white and vermilion.

By noon Denny was hungry, yet so overcome with nervous exhaustion that he almost decided to forego the midday meal. Aware, however, that an absence from two meals running would surely precipitate an intrusion by his father with the servant girl as proxy, he reluctantly left his room and went downstairs to face his father over luncheon.

Despite his complaisance, the father was immediately aware of the transformation in his son.

"Spring seems to have put new life into the lad," he said, turning over the page of a book. "You're like your mother in that respect and in that respect only, thank God. She never did do well in cold weather."

It was the first time he had mentioned the mother to the son since he had been forced to explain her departure obliquely some five years before. The boy was shocked. But as the opportunity had arisen, he hastily decided to follow up the mention of his mother. It was unseemly that he should disclose any sentiment, so he hesitated and calculated before putting his question. "Why doesn't she write or send me presents?" he asked.

His father's pause made him almost unbearably aware of the man's chagrin in having opened the subject. He didn't look up at the boy as he answered, "Because legally she is not allowed to."

The remainder of the meal was passed in silent and mutual embarrassment.

Denny returned to his room as soon as he could respectfully quit the table, and while unlocking the door for an awful moment the possibility that the moth might have escaped, might never really have been there, scorched Denny's mind. But it was there, almost as he had left it, only now it had changed its position; the spread of its wings being nearly horizontal and in this position Denny realized that the lamp chimney was too narrow to allow it free movement.

There was no receptacle in the room any larger and in Denny's mind there paraded the various jars, the vases, and other vessels in the house that had from time to time in the past served as enclosures for his specimens. None of them was large enough. Without sufficient room, the moth as soon as it attempted flight would in no time at all damage its wings. In a kind of frenzy Denny racked his brains for the memory of some container that would satisfy his need. Like a ferret his thoughts suddenly pounced on what had eluded them. In his father's room a huge crystal tobacco jar with a lid of repoussé silver stood on an ebony taboret beneath the smirking head of a tiger.

There was no time to lose; for within five hours after emerging from the cocoon a moth will try its wings in flight. Breathlessly Denny bounded down the stairs and for a moment only hesitated before he knocked upon his father's door.

"Yes?" his father asked querulously, and Denny turned the knob and walked in.

"Father—" he began, but he had not as yet caught his breath.

"Speak up, boy, and stop shaking. Why, even confronted by a rogue elephant I never shook so."

"I want to b-b-borrow something," the boy managed to stammer.

"Be more explicit! Be more explicit! What do you want? A ticket to Fall River? A hundred-dollar bill? A dose of ipecac? The last would seem the most logical, to judge from your looks."

Hating his father as he had never hated him before, the boy spoke up. "I want to borrow your tobacco jar."

"Which one?" the father parried. "The elephant foot the President gave me? The Benares brass? The Dutch pottery one? The music box?"

The boy could bear this bantering no longer. "I want that one." And he pointed directly where it stood half full of tobacco.

"What for?" his father asked.

The boy's bravura was suddenly extinguished.

"Speak up. If you make an extraordinary request you must be ready to back it up with a motive."

"I want it for a specimen."

"What's wrong with all the containers you have already appropriated from kitchen, pantry, and parlor?"

Denny would not say they were not big enough. It might arouse sufficient interest within his father so that he would insist on seeing for himself what this monster was. Denny had a vision of his father grabbing the moth and hastening to impale it upon the study wall, adding it to his other conquests.

"They won't do," Denny said.

"Why won't they do?"

"They just won't."

"Be explicit!" his father thundered at him.

"I want to put some stuff in it that won't fit in the others."

"You will stand where you are without moving until you can tell me what you mean by 'stuff.' " His father laid down his glasses and settled back in his chair to underscore the fact that he was prepared to wait all day if need be.

"Chrysalids and dirt and sticks and food for them," the boy mumbled.

The man stared at Denny as if he were an animal he had at bay.

"You intend to put *that* filth into *that* jar?"

Denny made no answer. His father continued.

"Are you by any chance aware that that jar was a gift from the Maharana of Udaipur? Have you any faintest conception of its intrinsic value aside from the sentimental one? And can you see from where you stand that, beside any other objections I might have, the jar is being employed for what it was intended for? And if for one moment you think I am going to remove my best tobacco from my best jar so that you can use it for a worm bowl you are, my lad, very much mistaken."

The man waited for the effect of his speech and then added, "Go and ask Ethel for a crock."

It was useless for Denny to attempt to explain that he wouldn't be able to see through a crock. Without a word he turned and walked out of the room, leaving the door open behind him.

His father called him back, but he paid no mind. As he reached the second landing Denny heard the door slam downstairs.

A half hour had been wasted and, as he had been sure it would, the moth, having gained control over itself, was in the first struggles of flight.

There was only one thing to do. Denny went to the corner where he kept his equipment. Returning, he lifted the lid from the lamp chimney, and reaching inside with his forceps he clenched the moth with a certain brutality, though he took pains to avoid injury to its wings. Lifting it out, the beauty of so few hours, Denny once again felt his omnipotence. Without hesitation he plunged the moth into the cyanide jar and screwed down the lid.

The wings beat frantically with the effort that should have carried the moth on its first flight through the spring air. Breathless, Denny watched for fear the wings would be injured. The dusty abdomen throbbed faster and faster, the antennae twitched from side to side; with a spasm the abdomen formed a curve to meet the thorax. The eyes, still bearing the unenlightened glaze of birth, turned suddenly into the unknowing glaze of death. But in the moment that they turned Denny thought he saw his distorted image gleaming on their black, china surfaces as if in that instant the moth had stored his image in its memory.

Denny unscrewed the cap, plucked out the moth and, piercing its body with a pin from the black paper packet, he pinned the moth to the wall at the foot of his bed. He gave it a place of honor, centering it upon a yellow willow tree. From his bed he would see it first thing in the morning and last thing at night.

A few days and nights passed, and Denny, though still on edge, felt somewhat as a hero must returning from a labor. The untimely death of the moth had perhaps been fortuitous, because now in its death the creature was irrevocably his.

The Cocoon

The meadows were already filled with cabbage butterflies, and Denny would go out with his net and catch them, but they were too common to preserve and so, having captured them, he would reach his hand into the net and squash them, wiping the mess in his palm off on the grass.

It was less than a week after the death of the moth when Denny was awakened in the night by a persistent beating on his windowpane. He jumped from bed, switched on the light, and peered outside. With the light on he could see nothing, and whatever it had been was gone. Realizing that though the light made anything outside invisible to him it would also act as a lure to whatever had tried to come in, he went back to bed leaving the light on and the window open. He tried to stay awake but soon fell back into sleep.

In the morning he looked about the room, but there was no sign of anything having entered. It must have been a June bug or possibly a luna moth though it had sounded too heavy for one, thought Denny. He went over to look at the moth on the wall, a morning ritual with him. Although he could not be sure, the dust of one wing seemed to be smudged and the oily stain from the body had soaked into the wallpaper considerably since the day before. He put his face close to the insect to inspect it more fully. Instinctively he drew back; the odor was unbearable.

The following night Denny left his window wide open and shortly before midnight he was awakened by a beating of wings upon his face. Terrified and not fully conscious, he hit out with his open hands. He touched something and it wasn't pleasant. It was yielding and at the same time viscid. And something scratched against the palm of his hand like a tiny spur or horn. Leaping from bed, Denny switched on the light. There was nothing in the room. It must have been a bat and the distasteful thought made him shudder. Whatever it had been, it left a stench behind not unlike the stench of the spot on the wall. Denny slammed the window shut and went back to bed and tried to sleep.

In the morning his red-rimmed eyes inspecting the moth plainly saw that not only were the wings smudged but that the simulacra of crabs and mouths upon the wings seemed to have grown more definite. The oily spot had spread still farther and the smell was stronger.

That night Denny slept with his window closed, but in his dreams he was beset by horned and squashy things that pounded his flesh with their fragile wings, and awakening in fright he heard the same sound as he had heard the previous night; something beating against the windowpane. All night it beat against the closed window and Denny lay rigid and sleepless in his bed and the smell within the room grew into something almost tangible.

At dawn Denny arose and forced himself to look at the moth. He held his nose as he did so and with horror he saw the stain on the paper and the crabs and the mouths, which now not only seemed more definite but also considerably enlarged.

For the first time in months Denny left his room and did not return to it until it was his bedtime. Even that hour he contrived to postpone a little by asking his father to read to him. It was the lesser of two evils.

The stench in the room was such that although Denny dared not leave the window open he was forced to leave the door from the landing into his room ajar.

What was left of the light in the hall below, after it had wormed its way up and around the stairs, crawled exhaustedly into the room. For some perverse reason it shone most brightly upon the wall where the moth was transfixed. From his bed Denny could not take his eyes off it. Though they made no progress, the two crabs on the hind wings appeared to be attempting to climb up into the two mouths on the fore wings. The mouths seemed to be very open and ready for them.

That night no sooner had the beating of wings upon the window awakened Denny than it abruptly ceased. The light downstairs was out and the room was now in darkness. Curling himself up into a ball and pulling the sheet over his head, Denny at length went off to sleep.

Sometime shortly afterward something came through the door and half crawled and half fluttered to the bed. Denny awoke with a scream, but it was too muffled for either his father or Ethel to hear because what caused him to scream had wormed its way beneath the sheet and was resting like a sticky pulp upon Denny's mouth.

Floundering like a drowning person, the boy threw back the covers and managed to dislodge whatever had been upon his mouth. When he dared to, he reached out and turned on the light. There was nothing in the room, but upon his sheets there were smudges of glistening dust almost black, almost purple, almost green, but not quite any of them.

Denny went down to breakfast without looking at the moth.

"No wonder you look ghastly," his father said to him, "if the smell in this house is half of what it must be in your room, it's a wonder you're not suffocated. What are you running up there? A Potters' Field for Lepidoptera? I'll give you until noon to get them out."

All day Denny left the window of his room wide open. It was the first of May and the sun was bright. As a sop to his father he brought down a box of duplicate specimens. He showed them to his father before disposing of them.

"Pugh!" said his father. "Dump them far away from the house."

That night Denny went to bed with both the door and window locked tight in spite of the smell. The moon was bright and shone all night unimpaired upon the wall. Denny could not keep his eyes off the moth.

By now both crabs and mouths were nearly as large as the wings themselves and the crabs were moving, Denny could swear. They appeared in relief, perhaps through some trick of chiaroscuro induced by the moonlight upon the dusty white and red markings. The claws seemed upon the verge of attacking the mouths, or were the so terribly white teeth of the mouths waiting to clamp down upon the crabs? Denny shuddered and closed his eyes.

Sleep came eventually, only to be broken in upon by the beating of wings against the windowpane. And no sooner had that ceased and Denny become less rigid than the thing was at the door beating urgently as though it must be let in. The only relief from the tap-tapping was an occasional, more solid thud against the panel of the door. It was, Denny guessed, caused by the soft and fleshy body of the thing.

If he survived the night Denny vowed he would destroy the thing upon the wall or, better than losing it entirely, he would give it to his father and he in turn

The Cocoon

would present it to some museum in Denny's name. Denny for a moment was able to forget the persistent rapping which had now returned to the window, for in his mind he saw a glass case with the moth in it and a little card below upon which was printed *Unique Specimen Lepidoptera. Gift of Mr. Denny Longwood, Aged 12.*

All through the night, first at the window, then at the door, the beating of wings continued, relieved only by the occasional *plop* of the soft, heavy body.

Though having dozed for only an hour or two, with the bright light of day Denny felt his decision of the night before indefensible. The moth smelled; that was undeniable. The matter of the crab and mouthlike markings seeming to expand and become more intense in their color could probably be explained by somebody who knew about such things. As for the beating against the window and the door, it was probably as he had at first surmised, a bat or, if need be, two bats. The moth on the wall was dead, was his. He had hatched it and he knew the limitations of a moth dead or alive. He looked at it. The stain had spread so that now its diameter was as great as the spread of the wings. It was no longer exactly a stain, either. It looked as if a spoonful of dirty cereal had adhered to the wall; it was just about the color of mush. It will stop in time like the others; just as soon as the abdomen dries up, thought Denny.

At breakfast his father remarked that the smell as yet hadn't left the house, that it was in fact stronger if anything. Denny admitted it might take a day or two more before it was completely gone.

Before the meal was over his father told Denny that

he was looking so badly that he had better see Dr. Phipps.

"How much do you weigh?" he asked.

Denny didn't know.

"You look," his father said, "all dried up like one of those pupae you had upstairs."

The moon shone bright again that night. In spite of his logic of the morning Denny felt sure that the movement of the white and vermilion crabs up to the white teeth and vermilion lips was more than just hallucination. And the beating of wings started at the window again. Then at the door. Then back to the window. And, in a way, worse than that was the *plop* now and then of the body against the barrier. Though he tried to rise and look out when it was at the window, his limbs would not obey him. Hopelessly his eyes turned to the wall again. The crablike spots clicked their tiny claws together each time the wings struck against the windowpane. And each time the plump, squashy body went *plop* the teeth snapped together between the thin-lipped mouths.

All at once the stench within the room became nauseating. There was nothing for Denny to do but make for the door while whatever it was still pounded at the window. As much as he feared and hated him, his father's cynical disbelief was to be preferred to this terror.

Denny refrained from switching on the light for fear that it would reveal his movements to the thing outside. Halfway across the room and shivering, he involuntarily turned his head and for a moment his feverish eyes saw what was outside before it disappeared.

Denny rushed for the door and unlocked it, but as he

The Cocoon

twisted the knob something beat against the other side of the door, pushing it open before Denny could shut the door against it.

When luncheon was over Ethel was sent upstairs to see what had happened. She was so hysterical when she came down that Denny's father went up to see for himself.

Denny lay in his pajamas on the floor just inside the door. The skin of his lonely and somewhat arrogant face was marred by the marks of something pincerlike and from his nose, eyes, ears, and mouth a network of viscid filaments stretched across his face and to the floor as though something had tried to bind his head up in them. His father had some trouble in lifting him up because the threads adhered so stubbornly to the nap of the blue carpet.

The body was feather light in the father's arms. The thought that the boy had certainly been underweight passed inanely through his father's mind.

As he carried his son out his eyes fell upon a spot on the wall at the foot of the bed. The pattern of a willow tree was completely obliterated by a creeping growth that looked like fungus. Still carrying his son, the man crossed over to it. A pin protruded from its center and it was from this spot, Mr. Longwood could tell, that the terrible smell came.

The Empty Schoolroom

by Pamela Hansford Johnson

*The young pupil's fawn-colored gloves
were in the piano.*

My mother and father were in India and I had no aunts, uncles or cousins with whom I could spend my holidays; so I stayed behind in the drab and echoing school to amuse myself as best I could, my only companions the housekeeper, the maid, and Mademoiselle Fournier, who also had nowhere else to go.

Our school was just outside the village of Bellançay, which is in the North of France, four or five kilometers from Rouen. It was a tall, narrow house set upon the top of a hill, bare save for the great sweep of beech trees sheltering the long carriage drive. As I look back some twenty-seven years to my life there, it seems to me that the sun never shone, that the grass was always dun-colored beneath a dun-colored sky, and that the vast spaces of the lawns were broken perpetually by the scurry of dry brown leaves licked along by a small, bitter wind. This inaccurate impression remains with me because, I suppose, I was never happy at Bellançay.

The Empty Schoolroom

There were twenty or thirty other girls there—French, German or Swiss; I was the only English girl among them. Madame de Vallon, the headmistress, did not love my nation. She could not forget that she had been born in 1815, the year of defeat. With Mademoiselle Maury, the young assistant teacher, I was a little more at ease, for she, even if she did not care for me, had too volatile a nature not to smile and laugh sometimes, even for the benefit of those who were not her favorites.

Mademoiselle Fournier was a dependent cousin of our headmistress. She was in her late fifties, a little woman dry as a winter twig, her face very tight, small and wary under a wig of coarse yellow hair. To pay for her board and lodging she taught deportment; in her youth she had been at the Court of the Tzar, and it was said that at sixteen years of age she was betrothed to a Russian nobleman. There was some sort of mystery here, about which all the girls were curious. Louise de Chausson said her mother had told her the story—how the nobleman, on the eve of his wedding, had shot himself through the head, having received word that certain speculations in which he had for many years been involved had come to light, and that his arrest was imminent. . . . "And from that day," Louise whispered, her prominent eyes gleaming in the candlelight, "she began to wither and wither and wither away, till all her beauty was gone. . . ." Yes, I can see Louise now, kneeling upon her bed at the end of the vast dormitory, her thick plait hanging down over her nightgown, the little cross with the turquoise glittering at her beautiful and grainy throat. The others believed the story implicitly, except the piece about Mademoiselle Fournier's lost beauty.

That they could not stomach. No, she was ugly as a monkey and had always been so.

For myself, I disbelieved in the nobleman; believed in the beauty. I have always had a curious faculty for stripping age from a face, recognizing the structure of the bone and the original texture of the skin beneath the disguisings of blotch, red vein and loosened flesh. When I looked at Mademoiselle Fournier I saw that the pinched and veinous nose had once been delicate and fine; that the sunken eyes had once been almond-shaped and blue; that the small, loose mouth had once pouted charmingly and opened upon romantic words. Why did I not believe in the nobleman? For no better reason than a distrust of Louise's information on any conceivable point. She was a terrible teller of falsehoods.

I was seventeen years old when I spent my last vacation at Bellançay, and knowing that my parents were to return to Europe in the following spring I watched the departure of the other girls with a heart not quite so heavy as was usual upon these occasions. In six months' time I, too, would be welcomed and loved, have adventures to relate and hopes upon which to feed.

I waved to them from a dormer window as they rattled away in fiacre and barouche down the drive between the beech trees, sired and damed, uncled and aunted, their boxes stacked high and their voices high as the treetops. They had never before seemed to me a particularly attractive group of girls—that is, not in the mass. There was, of course, Hélène de Courcey, with her great olive eyes; Madeleine Millet, whose pale red hair hung to her knees; but in the cluster they had no particular charm. That day, however, as, in new

The Empty Schoolroom

bonnets flowered and feathered and gauzed, they passed from sight down the narrowing file of beeches, I thought them all beautiful as princesses, and as princesses fortunate. Perhaps the nip in the air of a gray June made their cheeks rose-red, their eyes bright as the eyes of desirable young ladies in ballrooms.

The last carriage disappeared, the last sound died away. I turned from the window and went down the echoing stairs, flight after flight to the *salle-à-manger*, where my luncheon awaited me.

I ate alone. Mademoiselle Fournier took her meals in her own room upon the second floor, reading as she ate, crumbs falling from her lip on to the page. Tonight she and I, in the pattern of all holiday nights, would sit together for a while in the drawing room before retiring.

"You don't make much of a meal, I must say," Marie, the maid, rebuked me, as she cleared the plates. "You can't afford to grow thinner, Mademoiselle, or you'll snap in two." She brought me some cherries, which I would not eat then but preferred to take out with me in the garden. "I'll wrap them up for you. No! you can't put them in your handkerchief like that; you'll stain it."

She chattered to me for a while, in her good nature trying to ease my loneliness. Marie, at least, had relations in the village with whom she sometimes spent her evenings. "What are you going to do with yourself, eh? Read your eyes out as usual?"

"I shall walk this afternoon, unless I find it too chilly."

"You'll find it raining," said Marie, cocking a calculating eye towards the high windows, "in an hour. No, less; in half an hour."

She busied herself wrapping up my cherries, which she handed to me in a neat parcel with a firm finger-loop of string. "If it's wet you can play the piano."

"You've forgotten," I said, "we have none now, or shan't have till they send the new one."

Madame de Vallon had recently sold the old instrument, ugly and tinny, and with the money from the sale plus some money raised by parents' subscription had bought a grand pianoforte from Monsieur Oury, the mayor, whose eldest daughter, the musical one, had lately died.

"You can play on Mademoiselle Fournier's," said Marie, "she won't mind. You go and ask her."

"What, is there another piano in the school?" I was amazed. I had been at Bellançay for seven years and had fancied no corner of the building unknown to me.

"Ah-ha," said Marie triumphantly, "there are still things you don't know, eh? You don't have to do the housework, or you'd be wiser."

"But where is it?"

"In the empty schoolroom."

I laughed at her. "But they're all empty now! Whatever do you mean?"

"The one at the top," she said impatiently, "the one up the little flight of four stairs."

"But that's the lumber room!"

"There's lumber in it. But it was a schoolroom once. It was when my aunt worked here. The piano's up there still, though *she* never plays it now." Marie jerked her head skywards to indicate Mademoiselle Fournier upstairs.

I was fascinated by this information. We girls had never entered the lumber room because no attraction

The Empty Schoolroom

had been attached to it: to us it was simply a small, grimy door in the attic, locked we imagined, as we had never seen anyone go in or out. All we knew was that old books, valises, crates of unwanted china, were sometimes stacked up there out of the way. There! I have failed to make my point quite clear. I must try again. *There was no mystery whatsoever attaching to this room,* which is the reason why no girl had ever tried the handle. Schoolgirls are curious and roaming creatures; how better can they be kept from a certain path than by the positive assurance that it is a *cul-de-sac*?

Dismissing Marie, I determined to go and seek permission from Mademoiselle Fournier to play upon her pianoforte. Since the departure of the old one, I had missed my music lessons and above all my practicing; most of the girls were delighted to be saved a labor which to me, though I was an indifferent performer, had never been anything but a pleasure.

Mademoiselle had finished her meal and was just coming out upon the landing as I ran up the stairs to find her. I made my request.

She looked at me. "Who told you about the instrument?"

"Marie."

She was silent. Her brows moved up and down, moving the wig as they did so. It was a familiar trick with her when she was puzzled or annoyed. At last she said, without expression, "No, you may not go up there," and pushing me, hurried on downstairs.

At the turn of the staircase, however, she stopped and looked up. Her whole face was working with some unrecognizable emotion and her cheeks were burning red. "Is there *no* place one can keep to oneself?" she cried at me furiously, and ducking her head, ran on. When we sat that evening in the drawing room, in our chairs turned to the fireless grate, she made no reference to the little scene of that afternoon. I thought she was, perhaps, sorry for having spoken so sharply: for she asked me a few personal questions of a kindly nature and just before bedtime brought out a tin box full of sugared almonds, which she shared with me.

She rose a little before I did, leaving me to retire when I chose. I stayed for perhaps half an hour in that vast, pale room with its moth-colored draperies and its two tarnished chandeliers hanging a great way below the ceiling. Then I took up my candle and went to bed.

Now I must insist that I was a docile girl, a little sullen, perhaps, out of an unrealized resentment against my parents for (as I thought) deserting me; but obedient. I never had a bad conduct report from any of our teachers. It is important that this fact should be realized, so the reader shall know that what I did was not of my own free will.

I could not sleep. I lay open-eyed until my candle burned halfway down and the moon shifted round into the windowpane, weaving the golden light with its own blue-silver. I had no thought of any importance. Small pictures from the day's humdrum events flashed across my brain. I saw the neatly-looped parcel of cherries, the currant stain at the hem of Marie's apron, the starch-blue bird on the bonnet of Louise de Chausson, who had left Bellançay to marry an elderly and not very rich nobleman of Provence. I saw the leaves scurrying over the gray lawns, saw a woodpecker rapping at the trunk of the tree behind the house. What I did not see was the

The Empty Schoolroom

face of Mademoiselle Fournier upturned from the stairway. She never entered my thoughts at all.

And so it is very strange that just before dawn I rose up, put on my dressing gown and sought about the room until I found a pair of gloves my father had had made for me in India, fawn-colored, curiously stitched in gold and dark green thread. These I took up, left the room and made my way silently up through the quiet house till I came to the door of the lumber room—or, as Marie had called it, the empty schoolroom. I paused with my hand upon the latch and listened. There was no sound except the impalpable breathing of the night, compound perhaps of the breathings of all who sleep, or perhaps of the movement of the moon through the gathered clouds.

I raised the latch gently and stepped within the room, closing the door softly behind me.

The chamber ran halfway across the length of the house at the rear of it, and was lighted by a ceiling window through which the moonrays poured lavishly down. It was still a schoolroom, despite the lumber stacked at the far end, the upright piano standing just behind the door. Facing me was a dais, on which stood a table and a chair. Before the dais were row upon row of desks, with benches behind. Everything was very dusty. With my finger I wrote DUST upon the teacher's table, then scuffed the word out again.

I went to the pianoforte. Behind the lattice-work was a ruching of torn red silk; the candle stumps in the sconces were red also. On the rack stood a piece of music, a Chopin nocturne simplified for beginners.

Gingerly I raised the lid and a mottled spider ran across the keys, dropped on hasty thread to the floor and ran away. The underside of the lid was completely netted by his silk; broken strands waved in the disturbed air and over the discolored keys. As a rule I am afraid of spiders. That night I was not afraid. I laid my gloves on the keyboard, then closed the piano lid upon them. I was ready to go downstairs. I took one glance about the room and for a moment thought I saw a shadowy form sitting upon one of the back benches, a form that seemed to weep. Then the impression passed away, and there was only the moonlight painting the room with its majesty. I went out, latched the door and crept back to my bed where, in the first coloring of dawn, I fell asleep.

Next day it was fine. I walked to the river in the morning, and in the afternoon worked at my *petit-point* upon the terrace. At teatime an invitation came for me. The mayor, M. Oury, wrote to Mademoiselle Fournier saying he believed there was a young lady left behind at school for the holidays, and that if she would care to dine at his house upon the following evening it would be a great pleasure to him and to his two young daughters. "We are not a gay house these days," he wrote, "but if the young lady cares for books and flowers there are a great number of both in my library and conservatory."

"Shall I go?" I asked her.

"But of course! It is really a great honor for you. Do you know who the mayor's mother was before her marriage? She was a Uzès. Yes. And when she married M. Oury's father, a very handsome man, her family cut her off with nothing at all and never spoke to her again. But they were very happy. You must wear your best gown and your white hat. Take the gown to Marie and she will iron it for you."

The Empty Schoolroom

The day upon which I was to visit M. Oury was sunless and chilly. Plainly the blue dress that Marie had so beautifully spotted and pressed would not do at all. I had, however, a gown of fawn-colored merino, plain but stylish, with which my brown straw hat would look very well.

Mademoiselle Fournier left the house at four o'clock to take tea with the village priest. She looked me over before she went, pinched my dress, tweaked it, pulled out the folds, and told me to sit quite still until the mayor's carriage came for me at half past six. "Sit like a mouse, mind, or you will spoil the effect. Remember, M. Oury is not nobody." She said suddenly, "Where are your gloves?"

I had forgotten them.

"Forgetting the very things that make a lady look a lady! Go and fetch them at once. Marie!"

The maid came in.

"Marie, see Mademoiselle's gloves are nice, and brush her down once more just as you see the carriage enter the drive. I mustn't wait now. Well, Maud, I wish you a pleasant evening. Don't forget you must be a credit to us."

When she had gone Marie asked for my gloves. "You'd better wear your brown ones with that hat, Mademoiselle."

"Oh!" I exclaimed, "I can't! I lost one of them on the expedition last week."

"Your black, then?"

"They won't do. They'd look dreadful with this gown and hat I know! I have a beautiful Indian pair that will match my dress exactly! I'll go and look for them."

I searched. The reader must believe that I hunted all

over my room for them anxiously, one eye upon the clock, though it was not yet twenty minutes past four. Chagrined, really upset at the thought of having my toilette ruined, I sat down upon the edge of the bed and began to cry a little. Tears came very easily to me in those lost and desolate days.

From high up in the house I heard a few notes of the piano, the melody of a Chopin nocturne played fumblingly in the treble, and I thought at once, "Of course! The gloves are up there, where I hid them."

The body warns us of evil before the senses are half awakened. I knew no fear as I ran lightly up towards the empty schoolroom, yet as I reached the door I felt a wave of heat engulf me, and knew a sick, nauseous stirring within my body. The notes, audible only to my ear (not to Marie's, for even at that moment I could hear her calling out some enquiry or gossip to the housekeeper), ceased. I lifted the latch and looked in.

The room appeared to be deserted, yet I could see the presence within it and know its distress. I peeped behind the door.

At the piano sat a terribly ugly, thin young girl in a dunce's cap. She was half turned towards me, and I saw her pig-like profile, the protruding teeth, the spurt of sandy eyelash. She wore a holland dress in the fashion of twenty years ago, and lean yellow streamers of hair fell down over her back from beneath the paper cone. Her hands, still resting on the fouled keyboard, were meshed about with the spider's web; beneath them lay my Indian gloves.

I made a movement towards the girl. She swiveled sharply and looked me full in the face. Her eyes were all white, red-rimmed, but tearless.

The Empty Schoolroom 219

To get my gloves I must risk touching her. We looked at each other, she and I, and her head shrank low between her hunching shoulders. Somehow I must speak to her friendlily, disarm her while I gained my objective.

"Was it you playing?" I asked.

No answer. I closed my eyes. Stretching out my hands as in a game of blind man's buff, I sought for the keyboard.

"I have never heard you before," I said.

I touched something: I did not know whether it was a glove or her dead hand.

"Have you been learning long?" I said. I opened my eyes. She was gone. I took my gloves, dusted off the webs and ran, ran so fast down the well of the house that on the last flight I stumbled and fell breathless into Marie's arms.

"Oh, I have had a fright! I have had a fright!"

She led me into the drawing room, made me lie down, brought me a glass of wine.

"What is it, Mademoiselle? Shall I fetch the housekeeper? What has happened?"

But the first sip of wine had made me wary. "I thought I saw someone hiding in my bedroom, a man. Perhaps a thief."

At this the house was roused. Marie, the housekeeper and the gardener, who had not yet finished his work, searched every room (the lumber room, too, I think) but found nothing. I was scolded, petted, dosed, and Marie insisted, when the housekeeper was out of the way, on putting a soupçon of rouge on my cheeks because, she said, I could not upset M. le Maire by looking like a dead body—he, poor man, having so recently had death in his house!

I recovered myself sufficiently to climb into the carriage, when it came, to comport myself decently on the drive, and to greet the mayor and his two daughters with dignity. Dinner, however, was a nightmare. My mind was full so of the horror I had seen that I could not eat—indeed I could barely force my trembling hand to carry the fork to my lips.

The mayor's daughters were only children, eleven and thirteen years old. At eight o'clock he bade them say good night to me and prepare for bed. When they had left us I told him I thought I had stayed long enough: but with a very grave look he placed his hand upon my arm and pressed me gently back into my chair.

"My dear young lady," he said, "I know your history, I know you are lonely and unhappy in France without your parents. Also I know that you have suffered some violent shock. Will you tell me about it and let me help you?"

The relief of his words, of his wise and kindly gaze, was too much for me. For the first time in seven years I felt fathered and in haven. I broke down and cried tempestuously, and he did not touch me or speak to me till I was a little more calm. Then he rang for the servant and told her to bring some lime-flower tea. When I had drunk and eaten some of the sweet cake that he urged upon me I told him about the empty schoolroom and of the horror which sat there at the webbed piano.

When I had done he was silent for a little while. Then he took both my hands in his.

"Mademoiselle," he said, "I am not going to blame you for the sin of curiosity; I think there was some strange compulsion upon you to act as you did. Therefore I mean to shed a little light upon this sad schoolroom by telling you the story of Mademoiselle Fournier."

I started.

"No," he continued restrainingly, "you must listen quietly; and what I tell you you must never repeat to a soul save your own mother until both Mademoiselle Fournier and Madame de Vallon, her cousin, have passed away."

I have kept this promise. They have been dead some fourteen years.

M. Oury settled back in his chair. A tiny but comforting fire was lit in the grate, and the light of it was like a ring of guardian angels about us.

"Mademoiselle Fournier," he began, "was a very beautiful and proud young woman. Although she had no dowry, she was yet considered something of a *partie*, and in her nineteenth year she became affianced to a young Russian nobleman who at that time was living with his family upon an estate near Arles. His mother was not too pleased with the match, but she was a good woman, and she treated Charlotte—that is, Mademoiselle Fournier—with kindness. Just before the marriage Charlotte's father, who had been created a marquis by Bonaparte and now, by tolerance, held a minor government post under Louis Philippe, was found to have embezzled many thousands of francs."

"Her father!" I could not help but exclaim.

M. Oury smiled wryly. "Legend has the lover for villain, eh? No; it was Aristide Fournier, a weak man, unable to stomach any recession in his fortunes. M. Fournier shot himself as the gendarmes were on their way to take him. Charlotte, her marriage prospects destroyed, came near to lunacy. When she recovered from her long illness her beauty had gone. The mother of her ex-fiancé, in pity, suggested that a friend of hers, a lady at the Court of the Tzar, should employ Charlotte as governess to her children, and in Russia Charlotte spent nine years. She returned to France to assist her cousin with the school at Bellançay that Madame de Vallon had recently established."

"Why did she return?" I said, less because I wished to know the answer than because I wished to break out of the veil of the past he was drawing about us both, and to feel myself a reality once more, Maud Arlett, aged seventeen years and nine months, brown hair and gray eyes, five foot seven and a half inches tall.

I did not succeed. The veil tightened, grew more opaque. "Nobody knows. There were rumors. It seems not improbable that she was dismissed by her employer . . . why, I don't know. It is an obscure period in Charlotte's history."

He paused, to pour more tea for me.

"It was thought at first that Charlotte would be of great assistance to Madame de Vallon, teach all subjects and act as Madame's secretary. It transpired, however, that Charlotte was nervous to the point of sickness, and that she would grow less and less capable of teaching young girls. Soon she had no duties in the school except to give lessons in music and deportment.

"The music room was in the attic, which was then used as a schoolroom also. The pianoforte was Charlotte's own, one of the few things saved from the wreck of her home."

M. Oury rose and walked out of the ring of firelight. He stood gazing out of the window, now beaded by a thin rain, and his voice grew out of the dusk as the

The Empty Schoolroom

music of waves grows out of the sea. "I shall tell you the rest briefly, Mademoiselle. It distresses me to tell it to you at all, but I think I can help you in no other way.

"A young girl came to the school, a child; perhaps twelve or thirteen years of age. Her mother and father were in the East, and she was left alone, even during the vacations—"

"Like myself!" I cried.

"Yes, like yourself; and I have an idea that that is why she chose you for her . . . *confidante*."

I shuddered.

He seemed to guess at my movement for, turning from the window, he returned to the firelight and to me.

"In one way, however, she was unlike you as can possibly be imagined, Mademoiselle." He smiled with a faint, sad gallantry. "She was exceedingly ugly.

"From the first, Charlotte took a dislike to her, and it grew to mania. The child, Thérèse Dasquier, was never very intelligent; in Charlotte's grip she became almost imbecile. Charlotte was always devising new punishments, new humiliations. Thérèse became the mock and the pity of the school."

"But Madame de Vallon, couldn't she have stopped it?" I interrupted indignantly.

"My dear," M. Oury replied sadly, "like many women of intellect—she is, as you know, a fine teacher—she is blind to most human distress. She is, herself, a kind woman: she believes others are equally kind, cannot believe there could be . . . suffering . . . torment . . . going on beneath her very nose. Has she ever realized *your* loneliness, Mademoiselle, given you any motherly word, or . . . ? I thought not. But I am disgressing, and that I must not do. We have talked too much already.

"One night Thérèse Dasquier arose quietly, crept from the dormitory and walked barefooted a mile and a half in the rain across the fields to the river, where she drowned herself."

"Oh, God," I murmured, my heart cold and heavy as a stone.

"God, I think," said Monsieur Oury, "cannot have been attentive at that time . . ." His face changed. He added hastily, "And God forgive me for judging Him. We cannot know—we cannot guess . . ." he continued rapidly, in a dry, rather high voice oddly unlike his own. "There was scandal, great scandal. Thérèse's parents returned to France and everyone expected them to force the truth to light. They turned out to be frivolous and selfish people, who could scarcely make even a parade of grief for a child they had never desired and whose death they could not regret. Thérèse was buried and forgotten. Slowly, very slowly, the story also was forgotten. After all, nobody *knew* the truth, they could only make conjecture."

"Then how did you know?" I cried out.

"Because Madame de Vallon came to me in bitter distress with the tale of the rumors and besought me to clear Charlotte's name. You see, she simply could not believe a word against her. And at the same time the aunt of Marie, the maid, came to me swearing she could prove the truth of the accusations. . . . Three days afterwards she was killed in the fire which destroyed the old quarter of Bellançay."

I looked my enquiry into his face.

"I knew which of the women spoke the truth," he replied, answering me, "because in Madame de Vallon's face I saw concern for her own blood. In the other woman's I saw concern for a child who to her was nothing."

"But still, you *guessed!*" I protested.

He turned upon me his long and grave regard. "You," he said, "*you* do not know the truth? Even you?"

I do not know how I endured the following weeks in that lonely school. I remember how long I lay shivering in my bed, staring into the flame of the candle because I felt that in the brightest part of it alone was refuge, how the sweat jumped out from my brow at the least sound in the stillness of midnight, and how, towards morning, I would fall into some morose and terrible dream of dark stairways and locked doors.

Yet, as day by day, night by night, went by with no untoward happening, my spirit knew some degree of easing and I began once more to find comfort in prayer —that is, I dared once again to cover my face while I repeated "Our Father," and to rise from my knees without fear of what might be standing patiently at my shoulder.

The holidays drew to an end. "Tomorrow," said Mademoiselle Fournier, folding her needlework in preparation for bed, "your companions will be back with you once more. You'll like that, eh?"

Ever since my request and her refusal, she had been perfectly normal in her manner—I mean, she had been normally sour, polite, withdrawn.

"I shall like it," I sighed, "only too well."

She smiled remotely. "I am not a lively companion for you, Maud, I fear. Still, I am as I am. I am too old to change myself."

She went on upstairs, myself following, our candles smoking in the draft and our shadows prancing upon the wall.

I said my prayers and read for a little while. I was unusually calm, feeling safety so nearly within my reach that I need be in no hurry to stretch out my hand and grasp it tight. The bed seemed softer than usual, the sheets sweet-smelling, delicately warm and light. I fell into a dreamless sleep.

I awoke suddenly to find the moon full on my face. I sat up, dazzled by her light, a strange feeling of energy tingling in my body. "What is it," I whispered, "that I must do?"

The moon shone broadly on the great surfaces of gleaming wood, on the bureau, the tallboy, the wardrobe, flashed upon the mirror, sparkled on the spiraling bedposts. I slipped out of bed and in my nightgown went out into the passage.

It was very bright and still. Below me, the stairs fell steeply to the tessellated entrance hall. To my right the passage narrowed to the door behind which Mademoiselle Fournier slept, her wig upon a candlestick, her book and her spectacles lying on the rug at her side—so Marie had described her to me. Before me the stairs rose to the turn of the landing, from which a further flight led to the second floor, the third floor and the attics. The wall above the stair rail was white with the moon.

I felt the terror creeping up beneath my calm, though only as one might feel the shadow of pain while in the grip of a drug. I was waiting now as I had been instructed to wait, and I knew for what. I stared upwards, my gaze fastened upon the turn of the stairs.

Then, upon the moonlit wall, there appeared the shadow of a cone.

She stood just out of sight, her foolscapped head nodding forward, listening even as I was listening.

I held my breath. My forehead was ice-cold.

She came into view then, stepping carefully, one hand upholding a corner of her skirt, the other feeling its way along the wall. As she reached me I closed my eyes. I felt her pass by, knew she had gone along the passage to the room of Mademoiselle Fournier. I heard a door quietly opened and shut.

In those last moments of waiting my fear left me, though I could move neither hand nor foot. My ears were sharp for the least sound.

It came: a low and awful cry, tearing through the quiet of the house and blackening the moonlight itself. The door opened again.

She came hastening out, and in the shadow of the cap she smiled. She ran on tiptoe past me, up the stairs.

The last sound? I thought it had been the death cry of Mademoiselle Fournier; but there was yet another.

As Marie and the housekeeper came racing down, white-faced, from their rooms (they must have passed her as she stood in the shade) I heard very distinctly the piping voice of a young girl:

"*Tiens, Mademoiselle, je vous remercie beaucoup!*"

We went together, Marie, the housekeeper and I, into the room of Charlotte Fournier, and only I did not cry out when we looked upon the face.

"You see," said Monsieur Oury, on the day I left Bellançay for ever to join my parents in Paris, "she did make you her *confidante*. She gave to you the privilege of telling her story and publishing her revenge. Are you afraid of her now, knowing that there was no harm in her for *you*, knowing that she has gone for ever, to trouble no house again?"

"I am not afraid," I said, and I believed it was true; but even now I cannot endure to awaken suddenly on moonlit nights, and I fling my arms about my husband and beg him to rouse up and speak with me until the dawn.

The Ghost of Washington

Anonymous

Did the General think John Reilly was a spy?

It was early on Christmas morning when John Reilly wheeled away from a picturesque little village where he had passed the previous night, to continue his cycling tour through eastern Pennsylvania. Today his intention was to stop at Valley Forge, and then to ride on up the Schuylkill Valley, visiting in turn the many points of historical interest that lay along his route. Valley Forge, his road map indicated, was but a short distance further on. All around him were the hills and fields and roads over which Washington and his half-starved army had foraged and roamed throughout the trying winter of 1777-8—one hundred and twenty-six years ago.

It was a beautiful Christmas day, truly, and, as he wheeled along, young Reilly's thoughts were almost equally divided between the surrounding pleasant scenery and the folks at home, who, he knew very well, were assembling at just about the present time around a heavily laden Christmas tree in the front parlor. The sun rose higher and higher and Reilly pedaled on down the valley, passing every now and then quaint, pleasant-looking farmhouses, many of which, no doubt, had been built anterior to the period which had given the vicinity its history.

Arriving, finally, at a place where the road forked off in two directions, Reilly was puzzled which way to go. There happened to be a dwelling close by. Accordingly he dismounted, left his wheel leaning against a gatepost at the side of the road, and walked up a wretchedly flagged walk leading to the house, with the idea of getting instructions from its inmates.

Situated in the center of an unkempt field of rank grass and weeds, the building lay back from the highway probably one hundred and fifty feet. It was long and low in shape, containing but one story and having what is termed a gabled roof, under which there must have been an attic of no mean size. On coming close to the house, a fact Reilly had not noticed from the road became plainly evident. It was deserted. He saw that the roof and side shingles were in wretched condition; that the window sashes and frames as well as the doors and door frames were missing from the openings in the side walls where once they had been, and that the entire side of the house, including that part of the stone foundation which showed above the ground, was full of cracks and seams. At first on the point of turning back, he concluded to see what the interior was like anyway.

Accordingly he went inside. Glancing around the large dust-filled room he had entered, his gaze at first failed to locate any object of the least interest. A rickety appearing set of steps went up into the attic from one side of the apartment and over in one corner was a large open fireplace, from the walls of which much of the brickwork had become loosened and fallen out. Reilly had started up the steps toward the attic, when happening to look back for an instant, his attention was attracted to a singular-looking, jug-shaped bottle no larger than a vinegar cruet, which lay upon its side on the hearth of the fireplace, partly covered up by debris of loose bricks and mortar. He hastened back down the steps and crossed the room, taking the bottle up in his hand and examining it with curiosity. Being partly filled with a liquid of some kind or other, the bottle was very soon uncorked and held under the young man's nose. The liquid gave forth a peculiar, pungent and inviting odor. Without further hesitation Reilly's lips sought the neck of the bottle. It is hardly possible to describe the pleasure and satisfaction his senses experienced as he drank.

While the fluid was still gurgling down his throat a heavy hand was placed most suddenly on his shoulder and his body was given a violent shaking. The bottle fell to the floor and was broken into a hundred pieces.

"Hello!" said a rough voice almost in Reilly's ear. "Who are you, anyway? And what are you doing within the lines? A spy, I'll be bound."

As most assuredly there had been no one else in the vicinity of the building when he had entered it and with equal certainty no one had come down the steps from the attic, Reilly was naturally surprised and mystified by this unexpected assault. He struggled instinctively to break loose from the unfriendly grasp, and when he finally succeeded he twisted his body around so that he faced across the room. Immediately he made the remarkable discovery that there were four other persons in the apartment—three uncouth-looking fellows habited in fantastic but ragged garments, and a matronly-looking woman, the latter standing over a washtub which had been elevated upon two chairs in a corner near the fireplace. To all appearance the woman had been busy at her work and had stopped for the moment to see what the men were going to do; her waist sleeves were rolled up to the shoulders and her arms dripped with water and soapsuds. Over the tops of the tubs, partly filled with water, there were visible the edges of several well-soaked fabrics. To add to his astonishment he noticed that in the chimney-place, which a moment before was falling apart, but now seemed to be clean and in good condition, a cheerful fire burned, and that above the flames was suspended an iron pot, from which issued a jet of steam. He noticed also that the entire appearance of the room had undergone a great change. Everything seemed to be in good repair, tidy and neat; the ceilings, the walls and the door; even the stairway leading to the attic. The openings in the walls were fitted with window sashes and well-painted doors. The apartment had, in fact, evolved under his very eyesight from a state of absolute ruin into one of excellent preservation.

All of this seemed so weird and uncanny, that Reilly stood for a moment or two in the transformed apartment, utterly dumbfounded, with his mouth wide open and his eyes all but popping out of his head. He was brought to his senses by the fellow who had shaken him growling out,

"Come! Explain yourself!"

"An explanation is due me," Reilly managed to gasp.

The Ghost of Washington 233

"Don't bandy words with the rascal, Harry," one of the other men spoke up. "Bring him along to headquarters."

Thereupon, without further parley, the three men marched Reilly in military fashion into the open air and down to the road. Here he picked up at the gatepost his bicycle, while they unstacked a group of three old-fashioned-looking muskets located close by. When the young man had entered the house a few minutes before, this stack of arms had not been there. He could not understand it. Neither could he understand, on looking back at the building as he was marched off down the road, the mysterious agency that had transformed its dilapidated exterior, just as had been the interior, into a practically new condition.

While they trudged along, the strangers exhibited a singular interest in the wheel Reilly pushed at his side, running their coarse hands over the frame and handlebars, and acting on the whole as though they never before had seen a bicycle. This in itself was another surprise. He had hardly supposed there were three men in the country so totally unacquainted with what is a most familiar piece of mechanism everywhere.

At the same time that they were paying so much attention to the wheel, Reilly in turn was studying with great curiosity his singular-looking captors. Rough, unprepossessing-appearing fellows they were, large of frame and unshaven, and, it must be added, dirty of face. What remained of their very ragged clothing, he had already noticed, was of a most remarkable cut and design, resembling closely the garments worn by the Continental militiamen in the War of Independence. The hats were broad, low of crown, and three-cornered in shape; the trousers were buff-colored and ended at the knees, and the long, blue, spike-tailed coats were flapped over at the extremities of the tails, the flaps being fastened down with good-sized brass buttons. Leather leggings were strapped around cowhide boots, through the badly worn feet of which, in places where the leather had cracked open, the flesh, unprotected by stockings, could be seen. Dressed as he was, in a cleanly, gray cycling costume, Reilly's appearance, most assuredly, was strongly in contrast to that of his companions.

After a brisk walk of twenty minutes, during which they occasionally met and passed by one or two or perhaps a group of men clothed and outfitted like Reilly's escorts, the little party followed the road up a slight incline and around a well-wooded bend to the left, coming quite suddenly, and to the captive, very unexpectedly, to what was without doubt a military encampment; a village, in fact, composed of many rows of small log huts. Along the streets, between the buildings, muskets were stacked in hundreds of places. Over in one corner, on a slight eminence commanding the road up which they had come, and cleverly hidden from it behind trees and shrubbery, the young man noticed a battery of field pieces. Wherever the eye was turned on this singular scene were countless numbers of soldiers all garmented in three-cornered hats, spike-tailed coats and knee breeches, walking lazily hither and thither, grouped around crackling fires, or parading up and down the streets in platoons under the guidance of ragged but stern-looking officers.

Harry stopped the little procession of four in front of one of the larger of the log houses. Then, while they

The Ghost of Washington

stood there, the long blast from a bugle was heard, followed by the roll of drums. A minute or two afterward, several companies of militia marched up and grounded their arms, forming three sides of a hollow square around them, the fourth and open side being toward the log house. Directly succeeding this maneuver there came through the doorway of the house and stepped up the center of the square, stopping directly in front of Reilly, a dignified-looking person, tall and straight and splendidly proportioned of figure, and having a face of great nobility and character.

The cold chills chased one another down Reilly's back. His limbs swayed and tottered beneath his weight. He had never experienced another such sensation of mingled astonishment and fright.

He was in the presence of General Washington. Not a phantom Washington, either, but Washington in the flesh and blood, as material and earthly a being as ever crossed a person's line of vision. Reilly, in his time, had seen so many portraits, marble busts and statues of the great commander that he could not be mistaken. Recovering the use of his faculties, which for the moment he seemed to have lost, Reilly did the very commonplace thing that others before him have done when placed unexpectedly in remarkable situations. He pinched himself to make sure that he was in reality wide awake and in the natural possession of his senses. He felt like pinching the figure in front of him also, but he could not muster up the courage to do that. He stood there trying to think it all out, and as his thoughts became less stagnant, his fright dissolved under the process of reasoning his mind pursued. To reason a thing out, even though an explanation can only be obtained by leaving much of the subject unaccounted for, tends to make one bolder and less shaky in the knees.

The series of strange incidents which he was experiencing had been inaugurated in the old-fashioned dwelling he had visited after information concerning the roads. And everything had been going along in a perfectly normal way up to the very moment when he had taken a drink from the bottle found in the fireplace. But from that precise time everything had gone wrongly. Hence the inference that the drinking of the peculiar liquid was accountable in some way or other for his troubles. There was a supernatural agency in the whole thing. That much must be admitted. And whatever that agency was, and however it might be accounted for, it had taken Reilly back into a period of time more than a hundred years ago, and landed him, body and soul, within the lines of the patriot forces wintering at Valley Forge. He might have stood there, turning over and over in his mind, pinching himself and muttering, all the morning, had not the newcomer ceased a silent but curious inspection of his person, and asked, "Who are you, sir?"

"John Reilly, at your pleasure," the young man replied, adding a question on his own account: "And who are you, sir?"

Immediately he received a heavy thump on his back from Harry's hard fist.

"It is not for you to question the General," the ragged administrator of the blow exclaimed.

"And it is not for you to be so gay," Reilly returned, angrily, giving the blow back with added force.

"Here, here!" broke in the first questioner. "Fisticuffs under my very nose! No more of this, I command you both." To Harry he added an extra caution, "Your zeal in my behalf will be better appreciated by being less demonstrative. Blows should be struck only on the battlefield." To Reilly he said, with a slight smile hovering over his face, "My name is Washington. Perhaps you may have heard of me?"

To this Reilly replied, "I have, indeed, and heard you very well spoken of, too." Emboldened by the other's smile, he ventured another question, "I think my reckoning of the day and year is badly at fault. An hour ago I thought the day was Christmas day. How far out of the way did my calculation take me, sir?"

"The day is indeed Christmas day, and the year is, as you must know, the year of our Lord one thousand seven hundred and seventy-seven."

Reilly again pinched himself.

"Why do you bring this man to me?" Washington now inquired, turning to Harry and his companions.

"He is a spy, sir," said Harry.

"That is a lie!" Reilly indignantly interpolated. "I have done nothing to warrant any such charge."

"We found him in the Widow Robin's house, pouring strong liquor down his throat."

"I had gone inside after information concerning the roads—"

"Which he was getting from a bottle, sir."

"If drinking from a bottle of necessity constitutes being a spy, I fear our camp is already a hotbed," Washington somewhat sagely remarked, casting his eye around slyly at his officers and men. "Tell me," he went on, with sudden sternness, looking Reilly through and through, as though to read his very thoughts, "is the charge true? Do you come from Howe?"

"The charge is not true, sir. I come from no one. I simply am making a tour of pleasure through this part of the country on my bicycle."

"With the country swarming with the men from two hostile armies, any kind of a tour, save one of absolute necessity, seems ill-timed."

"When I set out I knew nothing about any armies. The fact is, sir—" Reilly started to make an explanation, but he checked himself on realizing that the telling of any such improbable yarn would only increase the hazardousness of his position.

"Well?" Washington questioned, in a tone of growing suspicion.

"I certainly did not know that your army or any other army was quartered in this vicinity." Reilly hesitated for lack of something further to say. "You see," he finally added, prompted by a happy idea, "I rode my wheel from New York."

"You may have come from New York, though it is hard to believe you came on that singular-looking machine so great a distance. Where is the horse which drew the vehicle?"

Reilly touched his bicycle. "This is the horse, sir, just as it is; the vehicle," he said.

"The man is crazy!" Harry exclaimed. Washington only looked the incredulity he felt, and this time asked a double question.

"How can the thing be balanced without it be held upright by a pair of shafts from a horse's back, and how is the motive power acquired?"

For an answer Reilly jumped upon the wheel, and at a considerable speed and in a haphazard way pedaled around the space within the hollow square of soldiers.

Hither and thither he went, at one second nearly wheeling over the toes of the line of astonished, if not frightened, militiamen; at the next, bearing suddenly down on Harry and his companions and making them dance and jump about most alertly to avoid a collision. Even the dignified Washington was once or twice put to the necessity of dodging hurriedly aside when his equilibrium was threatened. Reilly eventually dismounted, doing so with assumed clumsiness by stopping the wheel at Harry's back and falling over heavily against the soldier. Harry tumbled to the ground, but Reilly dexterously landed on his feet. At once he began offering a profusion of apologies.

"You did that by design!" Harry shouted, jumping to his feet. His face was red with anger and he shook his fist threateningly at the bicyclist.

Washington commanded the man to hold his peace. Then to Reilly he expressed a great surprise at his performance and a desire to know more about the bicycle. The young man thereupon described the machine minutely, lifting it into the air and spinning the wheels to illustrate how smoothly they rotated.

"I can see it is possible to ride the contrivance with rapidity. It has been put together with wonderful ingenuity," Washington said, when Reilly had replaced the wheel on the ground.

"It is but a toy," an officer spoke up. "Put our friend on his bundle of tin and race him against one of our horsemen and he would make a sorry showing."

Reilly smiled. "I bear the gentleman no ill will for his opinion," he said. "Still, I should like to show him by a practical test of the subject that his ignorance of it is most profound."

"You would test the speed of the machine against that of a horse?" Washington said, in amazement.

"I would, sir. You have a good road yonder. With your permission and a worthy opponent I would make the test at once."

"But, sir, the man is a spy," Harry broke in. "Would it not be better to throw a rope around his neck and give him his deserts?"

"The charge is by no means proven," Washington replied. "Nor can it be until a court martial convenes this afternoon. And I see no reason why we may not in the meantime enjoy the unique contest which has been suggested. It will make a pleasant break in the routine of camp life."

A murmur of approval went up from the masses of men by whom they were surrounded. While they had been talking it seemed as though everybody in the camp not already on the scene had gathered together behind the square of infantry.

"Then, sir," Harry said, with some eagerness, "I would like to be the man to ride the horse. There is no better animal than mine anywhere. And I understand his tricks and humors quite well enough to put him to his best pace."

"I confess I have heard you well spoken of as a horseman," Washington said. "Be away with you! Saddle and bridle your horse at once."

It was the chain of singular circumstances narrated above which brought John Reilly into the most remarkable contest of his life. He had entered many bicycle races at one time or other, always with credit to himself and to the club whose colors he wore. And he had every expectation of making a good showing today. Yet a reflection of the weird conditions which had brought about the present contest took away some of his self-possession when a few minutes later he was marched over to the turnpike and left to his own thoughts, while the officers were pacing out a one-mile straightaway course down the road.

After the measurements had been taken, two unbroken lines of soldiers were formed along the entire mile; a most evident precaution against Reilly leaving the race course at any point to escape across the fields. Washington came up to him again, when the preparations were completed, to shake his hand and whisper a word or two of encouragement in his ear. Having performed these kindly acts he left to take up a position near the point of finish.

The beginning of the course was located close to the battery of half-concealed field pieces. Reilly was now conducted to this place. Shortly afterward Harry appeared on his horse. He leered at the bicyclist contemptuously and said something of a sarcastic nature partly under his breath when the two lined up, side by side, for the start. To these slights Reilly paid no heed; he had a strong belief that when the race was over there would be left in the mutton-like head of his opponent very little of his present inclination toward the humorous. The soldier's mount was a handsome black mare, fourteen and a half hands high; strong of limbs and at the flanks, and animated by a spirit that kept her prancing around with continuous action. It must be admitted that the man rode very well. He guided the animal with ease and nonchalance when she reared and plunged, and kept her movements confined to an incredibly small piece of ground, considering her abundance of action.

"Keep to your own side of the road throughout the race. I don't want to be collided with by your big beast," Reilly cautioned, while they were awaiting two signals from the starter.

To this Harry replied in some derision, "I'll give you a good share of the road at the start, and all of it and my dust, too, afterward." And then the officer who held the pistol fired the first shot.

Reilly was well satisfied with the conditions under which the race was to be made. The road was wide and level, smooth, hard and straight, and a strong breeze which had sprung up, blew squarely against his back. His wheel was geared up to eighty-four inches; the breeze promised to be a valuable adjunct in pushing it along. Awaiting the second and last signal, Reilly glanced down the two blue ranks of soldiers, which stretched away into hazy lines in the distance and converged at the termination of the course where a flag had been stuck into the ground. The soldiers were at parade rest. Their unceasing movements as they chatted to one another, turning their bodies this way and that and craning their heads forward to look toward the starting point, and then jerking them back, made the lines seem like long, squirming snakes. At the end of the course a thick bunch of militiamen clogged the road and overspread into the fields.

Crack! The signal to be off. Reilly shoved aside the fellow who had been holding his wheel upright while he was astride of it, and pushed down on the pedals. The mare's hoofs dug the earth; her great muscular legs straightened out; she sprang forward with a snort of apparent pleasure, taking the lead at the very start. Reilly heard the shout of excitement run along the two ranks of soldiers. He saw them waving their arms and hats as he went by. And on ahead through the cloud of dust there was visible the shadow-like outline of the snorting, galloping horse, whose hoofbeats sounded clear and sharp above the din which came from the sides of the highway. The mare crept farther and farther ahead. Very soon a hundred feet or more of road lay between her and the bicyclist. Harry turned in his saddle and called out another sarcasm.

"I shall pass you very soon. Keep to your own side of the road!" Reilly shouted, not a bit daunted by the way the race had commenced. His head was well down over the handlebars, his back had the shape of the upper portion of an immense egg. Up and down his legs moved; faster and faster and faster yet. He went by the soldiers so rapidly that they only appeared to be two streaks of blurry color. Their sharp rasping shouts sounded like the cracking of musketry. The cloud of dust blew against the bicyclist's head and into his mouth and throat. When he glanced ahead again he saw with satisfaction that the mare was no longer increasing her lead. It soon became evident even that he was slowly cutting down the advantages she had secured.

Harry again turned his head shortly afterward, doubtless expecting to find his opponent hopelessly distanced by this time. Instead of this Reilly was alarmingly close upon him. The man ejaculated a sudden oath and lashed his animal furiously. Straining every nerve and sinew the mare for the moment pushed farther ahead. Then her pace slackened a bit and Reilly again crept up to her. Closer and closer to her than before, until his head was abreast of her outstretched tail. Harry was lashing the mare and swearing at her unceasingly now. But she had spurted once and appeared to be incapable of again increasing her speed. In this way they went on for some little distance, Harry using his whip brutally, the mare desperately struggling to attain a greater pace, Reilly hanging on with tenacity to her hind flanks and giving up not an inch of ground.

A mile is indeed a very short distance when traversed at such a pace. The finishing flag was already but a few hundred feet farther on. Reilly realized that it was time now to go to the front. He gritted his teeth together with determination and bent his head down even farther toward his front wheel. Then his feet began to move so quickly that there was only visible an indistinct blur at the sides of his crankshaft. At this very second, with a face marked with rage and hatred, Harry brought his horse suddenly across the road to that part of it which he had been warned to avoid.

It is hard to tell what kept Reilly from being run into and trampled under foot. An attempt at back-pedaling, a sudden twist of the handlebars, a lurch to one side that almost threw him from his seat. Then, in the fraction of a second he was over on the other side of the road, pushing ahead of the mare almost as though she were standing still. The outburst of alarm from the throats of the soldiers changed when they saw that Reilly had not been injured; first into a shout of indignation at the dastardly attempt which had been made to run him down, and then into a roar of delight when the bicyclist breasted the flag, a winner of the race by twenty feet.

As he crossed the line Reilly caught a glimpse of

Washington. He stood close to the flag and was waving his hat in the air with the enthusiasm of a schoolboy. Reilly went on down the road slackening his speed as effectively as he could. But before it was possible to entirely stop his wheel's momentum the noisy acclamations in his rear ceased with startling suddenness. He turned in his saddle and looked back. As sure as St. Peter he had the road entirely to himself. There wasn't a soldier or the ghost of a soldier in sight.

As soon as he could he turned his bicycle about and rode slowly back along the highway, now so singularly deserted, looking hither and thither in vain for some trace of the vanished army. Even the flag which had been stuck into the ground at the end of the one-mile race course was gone. The breeze had died out again and the air was tranquil and warm. In the branches of a nearby tree two sparrows chirped and twittered peacefully. Reilly went back to the place where the camp had been. He found there only open fields on one side of the road and a clump of woodland on the other. He continued on down the little hill up which Harry and his companions had brought him a few hours previously and followed the road on farther, coming finally to the fork in it near which was located the old farmhouse wherein he had been taken captive. The house was, as it had been when he had previously entered it, falling apart from age and neglect. When he went inside he found lying on the brick hearth in front of the fireplace a number of pieces of broken glass.